First published in 2005 by New Holland Publishers (UK) Ltd
London • Cape Town • Sydney • Auckland
Garfield House, 86–88 Edgware Road, London W2 2EA, United Kingdom
www.newhollandpublishers.com
80 McKenzie Street, Cape Town 8001, South Africa
Level 1, Unit 4, 14 Aquatic Drive, Frenchs Forest, NSW 2086, Australia
218 Lake Road, Northcote, Auckland
Copyright © 2005 text AG&G Books
The right of David Squire to be identified as author of this work has been asserted by him in
accordance with the Copyright, Designs and Patents Act 1988.
Copyright © 2005 illustrations and photographs New Holland Publishers (UK) Ltd
Copyright © 2005 New Holland Publishers (UK) Ltd
ISBN 1 84330 790 1
10 9 8 7 6 5 4 3 2 1
Editorial Direction: Rosemary Wilkinson Senior Editor: Clare Hubbard Production: Hazel Kirkman
Designed and created for New Holland by AG&G Books Copyright © 2003 "Specialist" AG&G Books
Design: Glyn Bridgewater Illustrations: Dawn Brend, Gill Bridgewater, Coral Mula and Ann Winterbotham
Editor: Alison Copland Photographs: see page 80
Reproduction by Pica Digital Pte Ltd, Singapore
Printed and bound in Malaysia by Times Offset (M) Sdn. Bhd.
The information in this book is true and complete to the best of our knowledge. All recommendations
are made without guarantee on the part of the authors and the publishers. The authors and publishers
disclaim any liability for damages or injury resulting from the use of this information.

Specialist

**The essential guide to selecting,
planting, improving and maintaining
trees and shrubs in the garden**

David Squire

Series editors: A. & G. Bridgewater

NEW HOLLAND

Contents

Author's foreword **2**

Author's foreword

Most gardens have several shrubs and a few trees and you may have inherited them with your garden or planted them when giving it a facelift. There are many shrubs and trees to choose from, and within this inspirational yet practical book we show their wide range, as well as ways to use them to improve and add style to your garden. Whether you want to add a colourfully leaved evergreen shrub to a border, perhaps to act as a beacon of interest throughout the year, or a tree that will create a focal point in a lawn, there are many shrubs and trees to capture your attention through their shape and colour.

For families with limited gardening time, shrubs and trees offer an easy way to a picturesque garden, although many shrubs need yearly pruning as well as regular check-ups. Looking after shrubs and trees is

described in detail, as well as their selection and ways to plant them. Once bought and planted, trees and shrubs create the opportunity of thrifty gardening, but with later opportunities to position other plants around them to produce even more spectacular features.

This all-colour book guides novice gardeners through the 'getting started' stage, as well as adding ideas which experienced gardeners will find useful. If you admire shrubs and trees, this book is an essential part of your gardening library.

SEASONS

Throughout this book, advice is given about seasonal tasks. Because of global and even regional variations in climate and temperature, the four main seasons have been used, with each subdivided into 'early', 'mid-' and 'late' – for example, early spring, mid-spring and late spring. These 12 divisions of the year can be applied to the appropriate calendar months in your local area, if you find this helps.

HEIGHTS AND SPREADS

The heights and spreads indicated for plants throughout the Plant Directory (pages 18–48) are those 15–20 years after being planted in good soil and in ideal conditions. Where shrubs grow in the protection of a wall, their growth will be slightly more.

Measurements

Both metric and imperial measurements are given in this book – for example, 1.8 m (6 ft).

What are shrubs and trees?

Shrubs and trees are woody plants that create long-term frameworks in gardens; shrubs live ten or more years and ornamental garden trees 20–50 years, and sometimes more. They are resilient plants, but require careful attention when planted and before fully established. Some shrubs need regular pruning to prevent an entanglement of old and unsightly stems, while trees require a yearly check to ensure that branches are safe.

Are shrubs and trees long-lived?

Shrubs create permanency in gardens. Here, the spiky Yucca, with creamy-white flowers, introduces a contrast in shape.

WHAT CAN SHRUBS AND TREES DO FOR A GARDEN?

Shrubs and trees are easy-care plants with many attractive qualities, including the following:

- **Colourful flowers:** many shrubs and trees create seasonal displays (see pages 18–27).
- **Colourful leaves:** both evergreen and deciduous shrubs and trees have coloured leaves (see pages 32–39).
- **Autumn-coloured leaves:** some deciduous shrubs and trees have leaves that assume rich colours in autumn (see pages 28–29).
- **Attractively shaped leaves:** some leaves are whole and perhaps round or oval, and others are finely dissected (see pages 28–29 and 32–39).
- **Coloured stems:** a few shrubs, if pruned yearly, produce colourful stems throughout winter (see pages 30–31).
- **Fragrant flowers and aromatic leaves:** these qualities are much desired in gardens (see pages 56–61).
- **Berries:** many colours and shapes (see pages 42–43).

Elaeagnus pungens 'Maculata' has an evergreen nature.

Prunus 'Kanzan' is deciduous, with flowers in spring.

Pyracantha 'Watereri' is evergreen and ideal as a wall shrub.

What are wall shrubs?

Many shrubs will grow very successfully against walls, as well as in borders in a garden.

- Tender shrubs prefer the warmth of a sun-blessed wall, especially in cold and exposed areas where otherwise they would be severely damaged or even killed.

- Space-saving is important in gardens, and by planting a shrub against a wall it is possible to save border space. Additionally, wall shrubs are able to utilize narrow spaces between walls and paths.

EVERGREEN OR DECIDUOUS?

Shrubs and trees are usually either deciduous or evergreen, although some can exhibit both characteristics, depending on the climate.

- **Evergreen shrubs and trees** – these retain a canopy of leaves throughout the year, but regularly shed and replace some of them. Most conifers are evergreen.

- **Deciduous trees and shrubs** – these shed their leaves in autumn, and then create a fresh array in spring. A few conifers are deciduous.

- **Semi-evergreen** – some shrubs, such as *Ligustrum vulgare* (Common Privet), that are normally evergreen can lose all or some of their leaves during very cold winters.

Range of shrubs and trees

Is there a wide choice?

A visit to a garden centre or nursery – as well as a glance through nursery and mail-order plant catalogues – soon reveals a wide range of shrubs and trees offered for sale. There are also many attractive conifers, some with a bushy and ground-hugging nature, and others that have a tree-like habit and eventually form dramatic focal points. There are shrubs and trees for all gardens, whatever their size. They will enthral you throughout the year.

CAREFUL SELECTION

Apart from pre-buying checks (see pages 8–9), it is essential that a shrub or tree will not rapidly outgrow its allotted position.

- The expected heights and spreads of shrubs and trees recommended in the plant directory (pages 18–47) are those 15–20 years after being planted in good soil and in ideal conditions. In mild areas, faster growth can be expected, but in cold and exposed places slightly less.
- Do not buy a shrub or tree that will eventually be too large for your garden. Even radical pruning will not help and may result in an unattractive shrub or tree that will have to be removed.

FLOWERING WALL SHRUBS

Growing tender flowering shrubs is made possible by planting them against a wind-sheltered wall and in full sun. Some of these shrubs, such as evergreen *Ceanothus*, have clusters of small flowers, while others, like *Fremontodendron californicum*, develop large flowers. The bushy and scrambling *Solanum crispum* (Chilean Potato Tree), which needs a trellis against a wall, creates a mass of purple-blue, star-shaped flowers with prominent yellow anthers during much of summer.

Evergreen shrubs

Flowers are attractive although invariably transient in their display, but the foliage of evergreen shrubs creates a display throughout the year. Some have the bonus of flowers, but even without this attribute they are attractive. Some, such as *Elaeagnus pungens* 'Maculata', have variegated leaves that drench borders in colour. Others are lower-growing and often carpet the soil in colourful leaves that help prevent the growth of weeds.

Illustration features *Choisya ternata*.

Attractive bark and stems

Trees with coloured bark, as well as shrubs with attractive stems, are very much welcome in winter and spring. Some are ideal on their own, such as *Acer griseum* (Paperbark Tree) and perhaps planted in a lawn. Others, like *Betula pendula* (Silver Birch), are superb when planted in a group and with small bulbous plants such as spring-flowering crocuses naturalized around them.

Illustration features *Cornus alba* 'Sibirica'.

Summer-flowering shrubs and trees

These are many and varied, with displays from single flowers to those massed on stems and forming plumes or balls. A few of these shrubs, such as *Philadelphus* (Mock Orange), have highly fragrant flowers and these are best positioned near to paths or edges of borders. Some summer-flowering shrubs have a low habit, while others like the renowned *Kolkwitzia amabilis* (Beauty Bush) grow up to 3 m (10 ft).

Illustration features *Brachyglottis* 'Sunshine' (also known as *Senecio* 'Sunshine').

Spring-flowering shrubs and trees

These create a wealth of colour; some are dramatic and bold, others demure and reserved. Some shrubs form a display packed with many small, separate flowers; others such as *Magnolia stellata* (Star Magnolia) have large and dominant flowers. Some spring-flowering shrubs need regular pruning – but not all. Forsythia, for example, needs yearly pruning to encourage the development of further flowering stems, whereas *Ulex europaeus* 'Flore Pleno' (Double-flowered Gorse) needs no regular pruning.

Illustration features an Azalea.

Evergreen and deciduous conifers

Some conifers are so large that they cannot be considered for planting in gardens, but fortunately many are suitable and are ideal as focal points. Most conifers are evergreen and those with coloured foliage are attractive throughout the year. Others are deciduous, with several having coloured leaves in autumn. A few deciduous conifers – such as *Larix decidua* (European Larch) – have beautiful young leaves in spring.

Illustration features *Cedrus deodara*.

Autumn colour

Autumn-coloured shrubs and trees are stunningly attractive, with leaves that reveal rich tints and shades before falling. When the weather is dry in autumn and a frost rapidly stops growth, the colours are rich and dramatic. Shrubs with magnificent colouring include *Rhus typhina* (Stag's Horn Sumach), with leaves that assume rich orange-red, purple and yellow tints. Trees include *Liquidambar styraciflua* (Sweet Gum) with rich orange and scarlet leaves.

Illustration features *Rhus typhina*.

GROUND-COVER SHRUBS

In addition to tall and dominant shrubs, some are superb at carpeting the ground with colourful leaves and, perhaps, flowers. Shrubs to consider include:
* *Calluna vulgaris*: there are many varieties to choose from, all with colourful foliage and flowers.
* *Euonymus fortunei*: there are several colourful varieties, with variegated, evergreen leaves.
* *Potentilla fruticosa*: this shrubby, deciduous shrub has massed stems and flowers throughout much of summer.

BERRIED WALL SHRUBS

Several shrubs with berries are superb when planted against a wall. *Cotoneaster horizontalis* (Herringbone Cotoneaster) has an aptitude for spreading horizontally as well as up walls. Pyracanthas are other ideal berried wall shrubs.

Winter-flowering trees and shrubs

Winter-flowering shrubs and trees are highly prized for their ability to bring colour to a season often considered bare and bleak. They range from ground-hugging shrubs to trees 1.8 m (6 ft) or more high. Position them where they can be readily admired, perhaps at the junctions of paths or as focal points further into a garden. They need little pruning.

Illustration features *Hamamelis mollis*.

Bamboos

Bamboos have stiff, hollow stems known as canes. They are usually planted in borders, side by side with shrubs and other plants; they also form attractive screens and hedges. Some create ground cover on banks and alongside rustic paths, while others stabilize steep banks. Many can be planted in containers on a patio or terrace, while they are essential parts of Japanese gardens – either planted in the soil or in containers.

Illustration features *Pleioblastus viridistriatus*.

Slow-growing and dwarf conifers

Many evergreen conifers remain dwarf throughout their lives, while slow-growing types planted when young are moved when they become too dominant. Dwarf ones are ideal for planting in rock gardens, and slow-growing types in heather gardens. Both slow-growing and dwarf conifers can be planted in containers when young and later planted into a garden.

Illustration features *Juniperus communis* 'Depressa Aurea'.

Shrubs and trees with berries and fruits

Berries and fruits introduce colour into gardens, especially in autumn, while some persist through to late winter. Botanically, berries are fleshy or succulent fruits and contain a number of seeds. To gardeners, the difference is usually of no matter. Birds, however, are usually more tempted by fruits than berries. Nevertheless, few berries escape the attention of birds, especially during long, cold winters.

Illustration features *Mahonia japonica*.

PALMS

Most palms are of tropical or subtropical origin. In temperate climates, unfortunately, there are only a few that are reliable outdoors – and even then in mild areas. Nevertheless, they are dramatic plants and introduce a Mediterranean aura to gardens. *Trachycarpus fortunei* (Chusan Palm) is the hardiest palm for growing in temperate climates.

Using shrubs and trees

Shrubs and trees are permanent, living parts of gardens and can be used in many ways. These encompass shrub and mixed borders, as hedges, windbreaks and focal points towards the end of a garden. They can also be planted as specimen trees in lawns, shaped into topiary figures and planted in containers. Shrubs and trees are versatile plants and create major, long-term features, throughout the year and for many years.

How can I use shrubs and trees?

PLANTING SHRUBS AND TREES

The time to plant shrubs and trees depends on whether they are container-grown, bare-rooted or balled. Additionally, whether they are evergreen or deciduous influences their planting. For detailed planting information, see pages 10–11.

TRANSPLANTING SHRUBS & TREES

There sometimes comes a stage in a garden's development when a shrub or tree needs to be moved. Occasionally it is better to buy a new plant but, where moving a shrub or tree is desired, see pages 16–17. Incidentally, if, when moving to a new house and garden you intend to dig up and take a plant with you, inform the new residents about your plans.

STOOLING

Stooling is an ancient woodland craft, involving cutting down shrubs and trees to encourage young shoots to develop around their base. Willow trees, for example, were cut back every winter to produce thin stems used in the making of baskets. The same technique is now used to encourage some shrubs to produce colourful stems (see page 67).

Mixed borders

Mixed borders, with their medleys of different plants – from shrubs and small trees to herbaceous perennials, bulbs and annuals – are the most popular borders in gardens. Because of their wide range of plants they are able to create interest throughout the year. For example, the winter-flowering *Hamamelis mollis* (Chinese Witch Hazel), with its golden-yellow, spider-like flowers, creates colour when most other plants are dormant and has the bonus of coloured leaves in autumn. At times when this shrub is not creating an attractive display, herbaceous, tuberous and bulbous plants provide colour.

Wall shrubs

Wall shrubs are ideal for clothing walls in colour and are especially useful in small gardens. Narrow borders between walls and paths can be planted with a wide range of wall shrubs, most of which benefit from shelter and warmth. Wall shrubs are not natural climbers and need to be pruned and shaped to enable them to blanket walls with flowers and leaves – and, perhaps, berries. Therefore, either a wooden trellis or a framework of wires secured to a wall is essential to give them stability throughout the year. If this support is neglected, strong wind or heavy snowfalls may dislodge them.

Shrubs in containers

Shrubs in containers create highly attractive features and have a wide range of flowers and leaves, some evergreen. The containers – encompassing tubs, large pots and Versailles planters – can be positioned on patios, terraces and around houses.

Additionally, they can be used in pairs to highlight the edges of entrances and windows. They are also excellent as defining features for the tops and bases of flights of steps. They can also be positioned to direct foot traffic.

Hedges

Hedges have many useful roles in gardens including – when planted as a boundary – the creation of privacy, reduction of road noise and preventing the entry of animals. Hedges also create attractive backgrounds for border plants and in earlier years were specially selected for colour-themed herbaceous borders. Internal and diminutive hedges, such as those formed of *Lavandula* (Lavender), are ideal for edging paths, while *Buxus sempervirens* 'Suffruticosa' (Dwarf Edging Box) is at its best in parterre gardens and with the more popular knot gardens, where the continuous interlacing of miniature hedges was an expression of an unchanging world.

PLEACHING

Pleaching is the creation of a hedge on stilts! The technique dates back several centuries, with lateral branches trained and pruned to form an interlaced screen. Traditionally, *Tilia* x *europaea* (European Lime) was used, but it attracts greenfly (aphids) and results in sticky honeydew falling and covering the ground. An alternative is *Tilia* x *euchlora* (Caucasian Lime), as well as *Carpinus* (Hornbeam) and *Fagus* (Beech). Wisteria, with its bonus of fragrant and colourful flowers, is another possibility. Plant trees 2.4–3 m (8–10 ft) apart, in two rows with 3.6–4.5 m (12–15 ft) between them. When trees have grown 3–3.6 m (10–12 ft) high, cut off the lower branches and train the upper ones along strong, lateral wires. Prune the framework of branches in autumn or winter. Summer pruning is also essential for Wisteria.

Windbreaks

Windbreaks help to create a plant-friendly garden, where strong and cold winds are not too much of a problem. Position the windbreak – formed of hardy evergreen conifers or deciduous trees – on the windward side of your garden. The influence of a windbreak – or a hedge – depends on its height. Where a windbreak is 6 m (20 ft) high, you can expect it to reduce the wind's speed by 65 per cent at a distance of five times its height, but by only 15 per cent at a distance of 20 times its height.

Specimen trees

Specimen trees planted in lawns help to give interest to a large area, as well as creating focal points of interest. Specimen trees range from the superb *Amelanchier lamarckii* (Snowy Mespilus or June Berry), with a profusion of white, star-like flowers in spring, to the leafy and deciduous *Acer platanoides* 'Drummondii', with distinctive white edges to bright green leaves.

Pyrus salicifolia 'Pendula' (Weeping Pear) is another superb specimen tree for planting in a lawn and, if planted in a round bed slightly larger than its weeping span, it can be highlighted by blue-flowered bulbs.

Topiary

Topiary is a popular way to grow and shape leafy shrubs and trees, and is a craft with a heritage that can be traced back more than 2,000 years. It is the art of shaping trees by frequently clipping and training them. Clipped *Buxus* (Box) was used during the first century AD to depict hunting scenes and ships, as well as to define names. Nowadays, topiary is usually devoted to creating simple shapes such as cones and spheres, as well as animals and birds, which were popular in cottage gardens. Such features never fail to draw attention.

Shrub borders

Shrub borders were traditional parts of large gardens, where borders were planted solely with shrubs that would create magnificent flower and leaf displays throughout the year. Nowadays, few gardens are large enough to have a single-theme feature and invariably shrubs are either combined with border perennials in 'mixed' borders or planted in small groups, alongside paths or in beds and corners. Rather than planting shrubs that are renowned just for their flowers, to extend the period of interest choose a medley of flowering and foliage types. Evergreen shrubs create colour throughout the year and many of them are featured on pages 32–35. Some are solely green, while others are variegated. Shrub borders can be given some added colour by replanting Daffodil bulbs (which earlier flowered indoors) between the shrubs.

Choosing shrubs and trees

Can I buy a shrub or tree at any time?

Nowadays, it is possible to buy a shrub or tree throughout the year and to plant it whenever the soil is neither frozen nor waterlogged – or the weather exceptionally cold. Container-grown plants have transformed gardening and, instead of gardeners being able to choose and buy a shrub or tree for only a few months of the year, plants sold in containers have made 'instant' gardening a reality at any time. Bare-rooted and balled plants are other ways to buy plants.

ADVANTAGES OF CONTAINER-GROWN SHRUBS

- **Plants grown and sold** in containers receive less of a check to their growth when planted than if 'bare-rooted', 'balled' or wrapped in polythene.
- **Container-grown shrubs** can be planted at any time of the year, when the soil is workable. However, spring and early summer are the best planting times because this enables tender plants to become established before the onset of winter.
- **Shrubs can be carefully inspected** before they are bought. This often makes the purchase more personal to you, especially if it is to be given as a present to a friend.
- **Poor-quality plants** can be rejected.

ADVANTAGES OF BARE-ROOTED SHRUBS AND TREES

- **Because they are grown in nursery beds**, their roots are not constricted in small containers. Relatively small plants do not suffer when grown and sold in containers, but the roots of large trees invariably become contorted and take longer to become established when transplanted.
- **Rarer and more unusual species** and varieties of trees and shrubs are not always sold as container-grown plants, but are available as bare-rooted types from specialist nurseries.
- **When comparing** like for like, bare-rooted shrubs and trees are usually slightly cheaper than container-grown types.

Where to buy

Always purchase shrubs and trees from reputable sources, as you will want to be assured about the plant's health, as well as it being correctly labelled. Apart from garden centres, nurseries and by mail order, there are other plant sources. Local shops and stalls in markets are possibilities – but always thoroughly inspect the plants.

Garden centres
Garden centres mainly sell container-grown plants and therefore it is essential to visit them in a car, although some centres offer a delivery service. Check out the garden centre as well as plants (see right); if it looks neglected and radiates little pride, this may be reflected in the quality of the plants.

Nurseries
Nurseries offer bare-rooted as well as container-grown plants. Container-grown types are available throughout the year, bare-rooted ones in winter. They can be collected, or arrangements made for their delivery. Some nurseries specialize in specific plants and it may mean a long journey or buying the plant through a catalogue.

Mail order
Many types of plants can be bought through mail-order sources, including bare-rooted shrubs, trees and roses, and container-grown shrubs and trees. Orders can be given by phone, fax or post, and paid by cheque or credit/debit cards. Most mail-order companies are reputable, but remember that you will be buying plants unseen.

HOW PLANTS ARE SOLD

Container-grown

✒ *Plants established and growing in a container – may be evergreen or deciduous shrubs or trees (for what to look for when buying, see opposite page).*

Bare-rooted

✒ *Deciduous shrubs or trees dug up from a nursery bed in winter, when bare of leaves (for what to look for when buying, see opposite page).*

Balled

✒ *Mainly conifers or small evergreen shrubs with hessian tightly wrapped around the rootball. They are usually sold during late summer and early autumn, or in spring.*

Wrapped in plastic

✒ *During their dormant period, deciduous shrubs, including roses, can often be bought wrapped in plastic. They are frequently sold through mail-order companies.*

WHAT TO LOOK FOR

Before buying or ordering a shrub or tree, check that it is suitable for your garden and will not, after a few years, become too large. It also needs to be right for your soil. Whether an evergreen or deciduous shrub, inspect it before buying. Such a check, however, is possible only with container-grown plants. For bare-rooted plants – and when buying through a catalogue – make sure the source is reputable and check that delivery dates are suitable.

EVERGREEN SHRUB

Check that the leaves are not torn or dead. Also, look above and underneath the leaves for signs of pests and diseases.

Stems should not be damaged, nor should they be congested.

The container should be clean and free from moss and algae. A clean pot usually indicates a healthy plant.

↗ Stand back from the plant and check that it has a well-balanced and even appearance, and is not excessively large for the container in which it is growing in the garden centre or nursery.

DECIDUOUS SHRUB

Deciduous shrubs produce new leaves each year and should be fresh and undamaged by pests and diseases.

Check the position of stems to ensure they are well spaced. Air should be able to circulate around the stems and leaves.

Matted roots inside the pot and showing out of the bottom indicate that the plant has outgrown its pot.

The top of the compost should be free from moss. There should be space between the compost and the pot's rim for water.

↗ Check that the plant has not been damaged by being positioned too close to its neighbour. Also, make sure that stems have not become misshapen through damage from strong winds.

GETTING PLANTS HOME SAFELY

When purchasing plants from garden centres, a car is usually essential. For safe arrival home with the plant, do not take children and dogs. Make a special visit to the garden centre rather than squeezing the plant between other items of shopping. Additionally, cover seats with plastic sheeting to prevent damage from loose compost.

TOOLS YOU WILL NEED

Planting shrubs and trees is not difficult and details of the techniques for both container-grown and bare-rooted plants are described on pages 10–11. In preparation for planting, gather together the following tools and equipment:
- **Hosepipe or watering-can** for watering container-grown plants the day before planting. Watering is also needed until the shrub or tree is established.
- **Spade** for digging out and replacing soil.
- **Garden fork** for loosening soil.
- **Straight bamboo cane or stick** for checking the level of the soil ball or roots.
- **Stout post** for supporting a tree.
- **Bucket of water** to ensure that roots of bare-rooted plants are kept moist.

WAITING FOR THE RIGHT TIME

Container-grown plants can be planted whenever the soil is neither frozen nor waterlogged. If conditions are not right, stand the container in a sheltered position on a firm surface. Keep the compost moist – but withhold water if the weather is extremely cold.

Bare-rooted plants need similar soil and weather conditions. For what to do if the weather is not suitable or the planting position is yet to be prepared, see right.

WHEN THE CONDITIONS ARE NOT SUITABLE

Bare-rooted plants sometimes arrive when either the soil or the weather conditions are not suitable for planting. Here is what to do.

- **Select a sheltered position** where the soil is moderately moist.
- **Dig a trench** 30–38 cm (12–15 in) deep, with a sloping side away from the prevailing wind.

- **Remove all packaging** and position the roots in the hole, with the main stem at a 45° angle.
- **Spread friable soil** over the roots and slightly firm it.
- **Lightly water** if the soil is dry.
- **Plants can be left** for several weeks until soil and planting position are suitable.

Planting and establishing shrubs and trees

How important is careful planting?

It is essential to plant a shrub or tree with great care and part of this is to ensure that the soil has been well prepared. This involves digging it several months earlier, breaking up the subsoil (especially if it is impervious to water), adding well-decomposed garden compost or manure and removing perennial weeds. Shrubs and trees become permanent parts of gardens and therefore deserve careful planting. Securely staking trees is also essential.

PERENNIAL WEEDS

Annual weeds such as Chickweed and Groundsel can be easily removed, but perennial types are more difficult. If left, stems and leaves choke plants and deprive them of water and food. Dangerous weeds include:
- **Bindweed:** twining stems and deep roots.
- **Celandine:** yellow flowers in spring, with spreading roots.
- **Couch Grass:** deep, spreading roots.
- **Ground Elder:** pernicious roots.
- **Horsetail:** upright, brush-like stems.

BEST SIDE FORWARD

Most shrubs and trees have a side that is more attractive than any other. When planting, check that it is facing towards the front of the border.

COMMON PROBLEMS AFTER PLANTING

Even when soil has been well prepared, perennial weeds removed and planting is a success, there can be problems in the early life of a newly planted shrub or tree.

- Dry weather for several weeks prevents the development of new roots. Thoroughly water the soil and apply a thick mulch (see opposite page).

- Rabbits can be a problem in rural areas; they gnaw at bark on the trunk and cause severe damage. As a preventative measure, wrap a plastic tree-guard around the trunk – they are inexpensive and quickly fitted.

- Wind dries out leaves and gusting wind rocks trunks of trees, loosening the roots. To prevent these problems, see right.

- Snow soon deforms shrubs and trees; gently brush it off.

- Double leading shoots appear on some conifers. Use sharp secateurs to remove one of them at the earliest opportunity.

PLANTING A CONTAINER-GROWN SHRUB

Container-grown shrubs can be planted whenever the soil is neither frozen nor waterlogged, nor the weather too cold. Ideally, the shrub should have roots that fill – but not excessively – the container and hold the compost firm.

Always ensure that the rootball is moist; the day before planting, stand the shrub (still in its container) on a firm surface and thoroughly water the compost. Allow excess water to drain. Additionally, water the planting area.

1 *Use a garden spade to take out a hole large enough to accommodate the rootball. Form and firm a slight mound in the base of the hole.*

2 *Remove the container and place the rootball on the mound. Adjust its height, so that the top of the rootball is slightly lower than the surrounding soil.*

3 *Firm soil in layers around the rootball. Use the heel of your shoe to firm the soil. Rake the surface level to remove footprints, then water.*

PLANTING A BARE-ROOTED TREE

Plant a bare-rooted deciduous tree during its dormant period, usually from late autumn to late winter. Check that the roots are not damaged; if necessary, use sharp secateurs to cut back broken and torn parts, as well as those that are thin or excessively long. Then, place the roots in a bucket of clean water for about 24 hours, so that they are thoroughly moist. If the tree was grafted, check that the union is firm and sound.

1 *Dig a hole large enough to accommodate the roots. Form and firm a mound; the old soil mark on the stem should be slightly below the level of the surrounding soil.*

3 *Carefully fit a tree-tie 12–18 mm (½–¾ in) below the top of the stake. Ensure that the trunk is held secure, but not constricted. Rake the soil level and gently water the entire area.*

2 *Knock a strong stake into the hole, so that its top is just below the lowest branch. Carefully draw friable soil over and between the roots; firm it in layers.*

STAKING AND SUPPORTING

Trees invariably need staking, especially when young and before their roots are established and able to give support. There are three main types of tree stake – vertical, oblique and H-shaped. Vertical stakes need to be put in place while the tree is being planted; if done when planting is complete, roots may be damaged. Oblique and H-shaped supports are put in place when planting is complete.

VERTICAL STAKES

➜ These are positioned on the windward side of the trunk. Fit a tree-tie 12–18 mm (½–¾ in) below the top of the stake and slightly below the lowest branch. For standard trees, fit another tree-tie lower down.

Wind direction

OBLIQUE STAKES

➜ The top of an oblique stake should face into the prevailing wind, with the top of the stake crossing the trunk about 10 cm (4 in) below the lowest branch. Use a strong but adjustable tie.

Wind direction

H-SHAPED STAKES

➜ These are formed of two stout stakes knocked into soil on either side of a trunk; secure a strong, horizontal support between them and about 7.5 cm (3 in) below the lowest branch. Secure the trunk to the horizontal support.

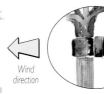

MULCHING

Mulches formed of well-decomposed garden compost or farmyard manure reduce moisture loss from the soil. They also add plant foods and reduce soil erosion during heavy rainstorms. Furthermore, a mulch both keeps the soil warm during winter and cool in summer, which encourages the presence of beneficial soil organisms. Mulching materials also include bark chippings which, initially and unless moist, are easily scattered by birds and wind. Peat was earlier recommended for forming a mulch, but its removal from peat-beds destroys the habitats of many insects, birds and plants. Peat is also used in some composts, but in limited amounts.

WIND PROTECTION

Until established, strong wind can push over trees and dry the foliage of shrubs. If the wind is persistent, small shrubs can be protected by the construction of a small, canvas screen secured by stakes on the windward side (see page 75).

Stake and tree-tie check

Regularly check that the supporting post is secure in the ground and is not rubbing against part of the tree. Additionally, throughout the year inspect each tree-tie to ensure that it is holding the trunk firmly but without constricting it. Most proprietary tree-ties can be easily adjusted.

Planting and establishing wall shrubs

Are wall shrubs difficult to plant?

The main problem for wall shrubs is that the soil near to a wall is often dry. Apart from the wall itself absorbing moisture from the soil, little rain falls close to it. Therefore, it is essential to position the roots of a wall shrub – or a climber – a reasonable distance away from the base of the wall. Invariably, the soil also needs careful preparation; mixing in bulky materials such as well-decomposed garden compost and manure will help it to retain moisture.

WHEN TO BUY?

Most wall shrubs are bought as container-grown plants and can be planted whenever the soil is workable and the weather not excessively cold. The choice of a wall shrub is usually a carefully considered buy, allowing sufficient time for supports to be erected or secured to a wall before planting commences (see opposite page for a range of supports). Some supports suit wall shrubs with a lax and informal nature, others become totally clothed with leaves.

BEST FACE FORWARD

It is essential that the best side on a wall shrub faces away from the wall. However, it is possible to cut away an unsightly stem if the rest of the shrub's 'face' is attractive.

Pyracanthas produce a wealth of berries during the winter months.

PLANTING A WALL SHRUB

During the months prior to planting, dig the soil and mix in plenty of well-decomposed garden compost or manure. Remove perennial weeds, taking care not to leave even the smallest piece of root. About a week before planting (and after the supporting trellis has been put in place) thoroughly soak the soil with water, covering a wide area. Then, the day before planting a container-grown shrub, water the compost in the container several times and allow excess moisture to drain. Watering the compost in this way will ensure rapid establishment for the roots.

1 Dig out a hole, deep enough to accommodate the rootball and with its centre 30–38 cm (12–15 in) from the wall. Add further well-decomposed garden compost to the planting area.

2 Form and firm a slight mound in the hole's base, remove the container and place the soil ball in position. Make sure the best side is facing outwards and dribble soil around the roots.

3 Firm the soil in layers, not all at once, using your heel. When the same level as the surrounding soil is reached, rake it level, water the soil and apply a mulch.

AFTER-PLANTING PROBLEMS

Until they are well established and their roots are absorbing moisture, wall shrubs will require regular inspection.

- If the weather is dry, regularly water the soil around the roots and for a couple of metres/yards on either side. It is no good just watering a small area, as moisture will be quickly absorbed by dry soil close to it. Add a further mulch around the shrub's base to conserve moisture.

- Ensure that stems are well secured to the supporting framework.

- Pests often linger and increase in plants growing in warmth provided by a sunny wall. Therefore, regularly check for pests such as greenfly which damage young shoots and suck sap from leaves. See pages 76–77 for problems from pests and diseases.

- Regularly check fixings for supports. Wind and rain – as well as frost – can soon loosen them.

COMPANION-PLANTING WALL SHRUBS

Mixing and matching does not have to be complex or expensive. Here are two associations to try:
- Position the deciduous *Cotoneaster horizontalis* (Herringbone Cotoneaster) close to *Jasminum nudiflorum* (Winter-flowering Jasmine), so that the yellow flowers of the Jasmine can mingle with the red berries of the Cotoneaster.
- Plant the yellow-flowered climber *Rosa* 'Helen Knight' close to *Clematis montana* (Mountain Clematis). They produce a feast of yellow and white in early summer. The Rose bears single, clear-yellow flowers amid small, light green leaves. The pure-white flowers of the Clematis are 2.5–5 cm (1–2 in) in width.

PLANTING A 'BALLED' SHRUB

Balled plants are mainly conifers or small, evergreen shrubs. They have hessian tightly wrapped around the soil ball and are usually sold during late summer or autumn, or in spring. Until the introduction of container-grown plants, most evergreen shrubs were sold 'balled'. Some shrubs are still occasionally sold in this state.

Ensure that the compost is firmed in layers around the roots, and not all at once.

When planting 'balled' shrubs
1 A couple of days before planting, thoroughly water the rootball. This is best done by immersing the rootball (still in its hessian wrapping) in a bucket of clean water. Leave it until bubbles cease to rise from the rootball. Then remove it and allow excess water to drain away.
2 Dig a hole that is large enough to accommodate the rootball, and then form and firm a mound in the base. Carefully remove the hessian and position the rootball on the mound.
3 Check the depth (slightly deeper than before), return the compost and firm it in layers around the roots.
4 Gently but thoroughly water the soil all around the shrub before applying a suitable mulch.

SUPPORTING A WALL SHRUB

Wall shrubs have woody stems and are therefore, in part, self-supporting. However, they need a framework to give stems support and protection against wind, snowfalls or heavy rain. Large shrubs, unless fixed, are likely to fall away from the wall if not supported. There are many types of supports, which are usually secured to a wall. Occasionally, independent posts with a supporting framework attached to them are useful, especially if the wall is not sound, or it is difficult to position a wall shrub close to a wall.

Method 1

↗ *A strong wooden trellis, perhaps formed of square-section battens, can be secured to a wall. Leave a space of 5 cm (2 in) between the wall and the trellis.*

Method 2

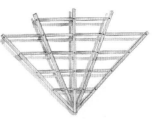

↗ *A trellis that spreads out is ideal for shrubs that are narrow at their base but widen towards their top. This design of trellis has a refined appearance.*

Method 3

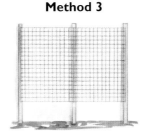

↗ *Stout posts knocked into soil about 23 cm (9 in) from a wall are ideal where a wall's surface is not sound. Secure strong, plastic-coated netting to the posts.*

Method 4

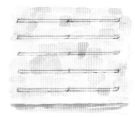

↗ *Galvanized wires that are secured to vine-eyes screwed into wall-fixings can be used to secure tiers of wires about 7.5 cm (3 in) from the wall.*

Planting hedges and windbreaks

Are hedges essential in a garden?

Hedges perform many roles in gardens. Boundary hedges form barriers, mark territory, create privacy, reduce wind speed, diminish road noise and prevent the entry of animals. Diminutive flowering hedges can be used internally alongside paths or, if small and leafy, such as *Buxus sempervirens* 'Suffruticosa' (Dwarf Edging Box), to form knot gardens. Tall, evergreen hedges are useful for creating attractive backgrounds for border plants.

DENSE AND IMPENETRABLE HEDGES

Some boundary hedges are especially suited for creating dense barriers.
- *Berberis darwinii*: evergreen, with small, glossy-green, prickly, holly-like leaves and rich orange flowers in spring.
- *Berberis* x *stenophylla*: evergreen, with arching stems bearing green, narrowly lance-shaped leaves. Golden-yellow flowers in spring.
- *Ilex aquifolium* (Holly): evergreen, with prickly, holly-like, deep green leaves.
- *Pyracantha rogersiana*: evergreen, with small, some-what spoon-shaped, mid-green leaves. White flowers in early summer and masses of berries.

WHEN TO PLANT

The times to plant evergreen and deciduous hedges are exactly the same as when planting shrubs and trees in borders.

Evergreen hedges

- **Container-grown plants:** plant whenever the soil is neither frozen nor waterlogged, and the weather is not exceptionally cold. The best time, however, is in spring, thereby giving plenty of time for plants to become established before the onset of winter.

- **Balled plants:** these are plants with roots wrapped in sacking. They are planted in late spring or early summer, or late summer and early autumn, when the soil is warm and moist but the weather not too hot.

Deciduous hedges

- **Container-grown plants:** plant whenever the soil is neither frozen nor waterlogged, and the weather is not exceptionally cold. The best time, however, is in spring, when there is plenty of time for plants to become established before the onset of winter.

- **Bare-rooted plants:** these are sold during their dormant period – when bare of leaves. They are dug up from a nursery bed and planted from early to late winter, whenever the soil is neither frozen nor waterlogged.

PLANTING DISTANCES

The distances between individual hedging plants depends on their vigour. Here are the spacings for a few popular hedges.

- *Berberis darwinii* (Darwin's Berberis): evergreen – 38–45 cm (15–18 in).

- *Berberis* x *stenophylla*: evergreen – 45–60 cm (1½–2 ft).

- *Buxus sempervirens* 'Suffruticosa' (Dwarf Edging Box): evergreen – 15–20 cm (6–8 in).

- *Escallonia* 'Donard Seedling': evergreen – 38–45 cm (15–18 in).

- *Fagus sylvatica* (Beech): deciduous tree – 45–60 cm (1½–2 ft).

- *Griselinia littoralis*: evergreen – 45–50 cm (18–20 in).

- *Ilex aquifolium* (Holly): evergreen – 45 cm (18in).

- *Lavandula angustifolia* 'Hidcote' (Lavender): evergreen shrub – 23–30 cm (9–12 in).

- *Ligustrum ovalifolium* 'Aureum' (Golden Privet): usually evergreen, but in exposed areas becomes partially evergreen – 30–38 cm (12–15 in).

- *Lonicera nitida* (Chinese Honey-suckle): evergreen – 30 cm (12 in).

- *Lonicera nitida* 'Baggesen's Gold' (Yellow-leaved Chinese Honeysuckle): evergreen – 25 cm (10 in).

- *Pyracantha rogersiana* (Firethorn): evergreen – 38–45 cm (15–18 in).

- *Rosmarinus officinalis* (Rosemary): evergreen – 38 cm (15 in).

- *Taxus baccata* (Yew): evergreen – 38–45 cm (15–18 in).

Internal flowering hedges

Several hedging shrubs have attractive flowers and are ideal as internal hedges.

- *Fuchsia magellanica* (**Hardy Fuchsia**): deciduous and slightly tender shrub, with a bushy nature and about 1.5 m (5 ft) high, depending on the area. Pendent, crimson and purple flowers from mid-summer to autumn.

- *Lavandula angustifolia* '**Hidcote**' (**Lavender**): evergreen shrub, 45–60 cm (1½–2 ft) high, with deep purple-blue flowers from mid-summer to autumn. (You might see this shrub listed in catalogues as *Lavandula nana atropurpurea*.)

- *Potentilla fruticosa*: deciduous shrub, 90 cm–1.2 m (3–4 ft) high when grown as a hedge, with masses of buttercup-yellow flowers throughout summer.

- *Rosmarinus officinalis* (**Rosemary**): evergreen shrub, about 1.5 m (5 ft) high when grown as a hedge, with mauve flowers in spring and sporadically through to autumn.

PLANTING A CONIFER HEDGE

Hedges created from container-grown conifers can be planted whenever the soil is neither frozen nor waterlogged, and the weather is not exceptionally cold. However, the best time is in spring. Choose healthy, equally sized plants, and on the day before planting thoroughly water the compost.

1 *Thoroughly prepare the soil, ensuring that all perennial weeds are removed – even the smallest piece will again develop roots. Stretch a garden line along the intended position for the hedge and use a spade to dig a trench about 30 cm (12 in) deep and 30–38 cm (12–15 in) wide.*

2 *With the conifers still in their containers, stand them in the trench and check that the top of each soil ball will be fractionally below the surrounding soil when planting is complete. Additionally, check that the individual plants are correctly spaced (see opposite page for spacings).*

3 *Carefully remove each container and stand the plants back into their positions. Carefully draw friable topsoil around the roots, firming it in layers rather than all at once (use the heel of your shoe). Take care not to push plants out of line as it spoils the symmetry. Water each plant.*

4 *Insert a strong bamboo cane on the windward side of each plant. Tie the main stem of each conifer to a cane; ensure that the stem is not constricted. In exposed areas, tie the top of each cane to a wire strained between a post at either end.*

AFTER-PLANTING PRUNING

The timing of pruning depends on the type of plant, whether evergreen or deciduous.

- **Coniferous hedges:** these do not need pruning until their leading shoots reach about 15 cm (6 in) above the desired height. Use sharp secateurs to cut off the tops.

- **Evergreen shrub hedges:** these are hedges formed of shrubs such as *Berberis darwinii* and *Pyracantha rogersiana*, and can be initially pruned in the same way as formal deciduous hedges (see below).

- **Formal deciduous hedges:** after planting, use secateurs to cut back each plant by a half to two-thirds. Additionally, cut back long sideshoots. This encourages the development of shoots low down, creating a thick base to the hedge. For later pruning, see page 68.

- **Informal deciduous hedges:** prune in the same way as for formal deciduous hedges. Many informal hedges are grown for their flowers and unless pruned when young the flowers may appear only high up.

PLANTING WINDBREAKS

Windbreaks, invariably formed of hardy, evergreen conifers, are positioned on the windward side of a garden.

- The influence of a windbreak – or a hedge – depends on its height. Where a windbreak is 6 m (20 ft) high, you can expect it to reduce the wind's speed by 65 per cent at a distance of five times its height, but by only 15 per cent at a distance of 20 times its height.

- Windbreaks inevitably impoverish soil at their base and make it impossible to grow plants close by. In a large garden this loss of space is not a drawback, but for a small area a large windbreak is impossible.

AFTER-PLANTING CARE

Until established, a hedge needs regular attention.

- Keep the base of the hedge free from weeds.
- During the first few months after planting, keep the soil moist – especially during dry periods.
- In spring of each year, refirm compost around plants.
- In spring, water the soil, add a sprinkling of a general fertilizer and apply a 7.5–10 cm (3–4 in) thick mulch around each plant.
- Regularly check that the ties securing stems to canes are not causing constriction; readjust as necessary.
- Eventually, the canes and wire can be removed – but first ensure that the hedge is established and growing strongly.

Creating an artificial screen

While a garden is becoming established – and especially if it is in a windswept and exposed area – a screen formed of a latticework of strong strips of wood attached to secure supports will make the area more comfortable for plants. Such a screen has several advantages over a hedge – it can be rapidly constructed, as well as quickly removed once the plants are established and growing strongly.

Heeling-in plants

If bare-rooted deciduous hedging plants arrive when the planting area has yet to be prepared – or when the soil is frozen or waterlogged – they can be heeled-in. This involves digging a 30–38 cm (12–15 in) trench in an out-of-the-way corner, with one side sloping at a 45° angle, away from the prevailing wind.

Place the roots of each plant in the trench, with the trunk or stems lying at an angle, and then spread friable soil over the roots. Lightly firm the soil around them, and then water the entire area. The plants can be left in the trench like this for several weeks – but you should always plant them out at the earliest possible opportunity.

Transplanting shrubs and trees

Why move a shrub or tree?

Shrubs and small trees sometimes need to be moved, especially when you are taking over or replanning an existing garden. Moving an established shrub or tree is neither quick nor easy, but if a plant is special to you – perhaps planted to commemorate a birth, wedding or other anniversary – it is a job well worth tackling. However, remember that the larger the plant, the greater the preparation needed to ensure that the tree or shrub transplants successfully.

WHEN TO MOVE SHRUBS AND TREES

The time of the year to move a shrub or tree depends on its nature – whether it is deciduous or evergreen.

• **Deciduous shrubs and trees:** these are best moved when they are dormant and free from leaves, which is at any time from late autumn to late winter, but depending on the mildness or severity of the season. However, remember to avoid times when the soil is frozen or waterlogged, or when the weather is exceptionally cold.

• **Evergreen shrubs and trees:** these are moved when the soil is warm yet the weather is neither exceptionally hot nor very cold. Therefore, the best times are in late spring and early summer, or late summer and early autumn.

POINTS TO CONSIDER

Size and age

Old and large shrubs and trees are more difficult to move and re-establish than small ones. For this reason, it may take three seasons to move a large shrub or tree (see opposite page for details), and a further season for it to become fully established. A healthy plant transplants better than a weak one. Therefore, in the year before moving, feed the plant with a general fertilizer.

Better to buy another plant?

Often a shrub or tree is so old and neglected that it is better to replant with a new one. Dig it out in autumn, add fresh soil to the area and leave throughout winter for the ground to settle. In spring, dust the soil with a general fertilizer to encourage the rapid formation of new roots. Then you can replant with a new variety of shrub or tree.

Is it a team job?

There is no doubt that moving a large shrub or tree is difficult for one person. The initial digging around a plant can frequently be managed by one person, yet the final digging under the shrub or tree and moving it is better undertaken as a team job. When helped by a 'novice' team, explain what is going to happen before embarking on the task, in order to minimize disagreements.

Are large plants difficult to establish?

Large shrubs and trees are difficult to re-establish because of the often disproportionately large amount of branch and leaf growth to the size of the rootball. Pre-moving as well as after-moving treatments can help (see right). If you are in any doubt at all as to whether a large shrub or tree can successfully be moved, it is better to replace it with a young plant.

Pre-moving treatment

Cut back large branches and excessive leaf growth to reduce the amount of water the roots will need to absorb after the shrub or tree has been moved. Additionally, for large shrubs and trees, cut a trench around the plant (see opposite page). This encourages the formation of fibrous, moisture-absorbing roots, which are essential for a plant's rapid establishment.

After-moving treatment

After planting, check that soil is firmly held around the roots. The action of frost loosens soil so firming may have to be repeated each spring for a couple of years. Other plant-establishing tasks include keeping the soil moist, adding a mulch, syringing the foliage and constructing a screen to reduce the wind's speed around the shrub or tree (see opposite page for full details).

MOVING A LARGE SHRUB

Large trees and shrubs are best moved over 2–3 seasons.

1 *In the first year, dig around and under half of the plant; replace and firm the soil. In the second year, do the same to the other side. During the third year, dig under the complete plant and move it.*

2 *With help, drag or lift the rootball on to sacking or strong polythene. Sometimes, it is possible to push strong planks of wood under the plant and to drag the rootball – plus sacking or polythene – along it.*

3 *Dig a large hole – with one sloping side – and fork over the base. Position the plant in the hole and, using a straight stick, check that it is deep enough to fit the roots.*

4 *Ensure that the plant's 'face' side is towards the front of the border. Draw and firm friable soil in layers around the roots; firm with your heel. Thoroughly water the soil.*

MORE TRANSPLANTING TECHNIQUES

- **Keeping the soil moist:** throughout summer, keep the compost around a transplanted shrub or tree moist, but not waterlogged. There is a careful judgement to be made about adding further water, because the roots will not be absorbing moisture until a shrub or tree is again growing.
- **Adding a mulch:** after thoroughly watering the soil, add a 7.5–10 cm (3–4 in) thick mulch over the ground to reduce water loss.
- **Sacking:** during periods of warm weather and after transplanting a small evergreen shrub, place damp sacking over the foliage to reduce water loss and the need for roots to absorb moisture.
- **Syringing:** regularly spray the foliage of evergreen shrubs to reduce water loss. However, do not do this in strong sunlight.
- **Wind screens:** a canvas screen, supported and kept in place by 4–5 stout canes and positioned on the windward side of an evergreen shrub, will reduce the loss of moisture from the leaves.

EASY MOVERS

Shrubs and trees with fibrous roots, such as Rhododendrons and Heathers, are easier to transplant than trees with a few large roots. Many trees have several major roots, and cutting these during pre-moving treatment (see opposite) encourages the formation of further roots.

In windy areas

Tall trees are at risk when being transplanted. As soon as the move is complete, secure the trunk so that it cannot rock and loosen the roots. There are several ways to tackle this job:

Never underestimate the buffeting and root-loosening ability of strong wind, especially during winter. Always secure the trunk firmly.

Use an oblique stake
Insert a long stake, with the lower end knocked into the ground at a 45° angle and its top towards the prevailing wind. Where they cross, use a strong, proprietary 'tie' to secure the stake to the trunk without causing constriction.

H-shaped supports are ideal where a tree is replanted in a lawn, as the grass can be cut close up to the tree's trunk.

H-shaped supports
Knock two stakes, vertically and about 45 cm (18 in) apart, into soil on opposite sides of the trunk. Tie a strong piece of timber between the two posts and close to the trunk. Then, using a proprietary 'tie', secure the trunk to the cross-member.

Maypole guys
Tie a piece of strong, car inner-tube around the trunk and just below the lowest branch, preferably about 1.2 m (4 ft) high. To this, tie four strong ropes or thick, plastic-coated wire and use strong pegs to secure them into the ground around the trunk.

Winter-flowering shrubs & trees

Are these plants difficult to grow?

Winter-flowering shrubs and trees are some of the easiest plants to look after, and once established require little attention. In addition, most of them need very little pruning. They can be planted in 'winter gardens' or in 'mixed borders' with herbaceous and other plants. Wherever they are planted, ensure that an all-weather path passes close to them, so that they can be readily admired without the need to cross a border or frost-covered lawn.

ADDED WINTER COLOUR

As well as winter-flowering plants for this season, remember the value of evergreen foliage. Consider using variegated evergreen shrubs as backgrounds; they provide a wide range of shapes and sizes.

Additionally, variegated evergreen climbers such as *Hedera colchica* 'Sulphur Heart' will soon smother the ground with colour. This eye-catching Ivy has large leaves that are boldly marked with an irregular central, yellow splash. Even though it has a vigorous, sprawling and spreading habit, it can be kept in check by pruning off any long shoots in spring or autumn.

There are also many varieties of *Calluna vulgaris* (Heather) which have attractive foliage – see page 32 for a description of *Calluna vulgaris* 'Gold Haze'.

Hamamelis mollis 'Goldcrest'

Viburnum tinus

Erica carnea

This colour- and shape-contrasting medley of shrubs will create interest during the winter season, and will continue to do so for many years.

Chimonanthus praecox
Winter Sweet (UK/USA)

Also known as *Chimonanthus fragrans*, this bushy, deciduous shrub bears spicy-scented, cup-shaped flowers with waxy, yellow petals and purple centres from mid- to late winter. The flowers are borne on bare stems.

Soil and position: well-drained soil and a warm position; preferably, in cold areas, plant against a sheltered wall.

Pruning: little pruning is needed, other than thinning out congested and old shoots in spring, after the flowers fade.

↕ 1.8–2.4 m (6–8 ft) ↔ 1.8–2.4 m (6–8 ft)

Cornus mas
Cornelian Cherry (UK/USA)
Sorbet (USA)

Hardy, densely branched and twiggy deciduous shrub with small clusters of golden-yellow flowers borne on naked stems from mid-winter to spring. Occasionally, shrubs bear edible, red, semi-translucent fruits. During autumn, the leaves turn rich reddish-purple.

Soil and position: fertile, moisture-retentive but well-drained soil in full sun.

Pruning: no regular pruning is needed, other than cutting out damaged shoots in spring.

↕ 2.4–3.6 m (8–12 ft) ↔ 1.8–3 m (6–10 ft)

Daphne mezereum
February Daphne (USA)
Mezereon (UK/USA)
Mezereum (UK/USA)

Hardy, deciduous shrub with purple-red, fragrant flowers from late winter to spring. They cluster on stems and are followed in autumn by poisonous, scarlet berries. There is a white-flowered form.

Soil and position: moisture-retentive but well-drained soil in full sun or light shade. It is suitable for chalky soils.

Pruning: no regular pruning is needed, other than cutting out damaged or misplaced shoots in spring.

↕ 90 cm–1.5 m (3–5 ft) ↔ 60–90 cm (2–3 ft)

Erica carnea

Erica (UK) **Heather** (UK)
Snow Heather (UK/USA)

Hardy, prostrate or low-growing evergreen shrub with terminal clusters of white, pink, red or purple flowers from late autumn to late spring. Wide range of varieties.

Soil and position: most Heathers require peaty, acid, moisture-retentive soil, but *Erica carnea* also grows well in chalky soil. Plant them in open, sunny positions.

Pruning: clip off dead flowers in spring.

5–30 cm (2–12 in) ⟷ 15–60 cm (6–24 in)

Hamamelis mollis

Chinese Witch Hazel (UK/USA)

Hardy, deciduous shrub or small tree with spreading branches. During early and mid-winter it bears sweetly scented, spider-like, golden-yellow flowers on naked stems. In autumn, the leaves assume rich-yellow shades.

Soil and position: moisture-retentive but well-drained neutral or slightly acid soil and a sheltered, sunny or slightly shaded position.

Pruning: no regular pruning is needed, other than cutting out straggly or damaged branches in spring.

1.8–3 m (6–10 ft) ⟷ 2.1–3 m (7–10 ft)

Mahonia x media 'Charity'

Hardy, evergreen shrub with leathery leaves formed of spine-edged leaflets. From early to late winter it bears semi-cascading, 23–30 cm (9–12 in) long spires of fragrant, deep lemon-yellow flowers.

Soil and position: moisture-retentive but well-drained, preferably slightly acid and peaty soil, although it also grows in neutral soil. It grows well in dappled light, as well as sun or partial shade.

Pruning: little pruning is needed, other than cutting back straggly stems in spring.

1.8–2.4 m (6–8 ft) ⟷ 1.5–2.1 m (5–7 ft)

Viburnum tinus

Laurustinus (UK/USA)

Hardy, dense, evergreen shrub with flat heads, up to 10 cm (4 in) wide, packed with white flowers from early winter to late spring. When in bud the flowers are pink. The form 'Eve Price' has carmine buds and pink-tinged white flowers.

Soil and position: fertile, deeply prepared, moisture-retentive soil and a sheltered position.

Pruning: no regular pruning is needed, other than cutting out dead, weak and straggly shoots in spring.

2.1–2.7 m (7–9 ft) ⟷ 1.5–2.1 m (5–7 ft)

OTHERS TO CONSIDER

- *Calluna vulgaris* **(Heather/Ling/Scotch Heather):** hardy, low-growing, evergreen shrub with flowers from mid-summer to early winter – sometimes later, depending on the variety.
- *Daphne odora* **(Winter Daphne):** slightly tender, lax, evergreen shrub with pale purple flowers from mid-winter to mid-spring. 'Aureomarginata' has leaves with creamy-white edges and is slightly hardier.
- *Erica* x *darleyensis* **(Erica/Heather):** hardy, evergreen shrub with clusters of flowers from early winter to late spring, in a range of colours including white, pink and purple.
- *Erica lusitanica*: large, evergreen shrub, up to 3 m (10 ft) high, with bright apple-green leaves and pink flower buds in early winter, opening to white. They usually last until late spring, or later. Even when damaged by frost, this shrub usually recovers.
- *Lonicera fragrantissima*: bushy, partially evergreen shrub. Fragrant, creamy-white flowers from mid-winter to early spring.
- *Lonicera standishii*: hardy, deciduous shrub with creamy-white flowers that open from early winter to early spring. It is free-flowering and is similar to *Lonicera fragrantissima*. Oval, mid-green leaves during summer.
- *Mahonia japonica*: hardy, evergreen shrub with lily-of-the-valley-scented, lemon-yellow flowers from mid-winter to early spring.
- *Mahonia japonica* **Bealei Group:** also known as *Mahonia* 'Bealei', this hardy, slow-growing evergreen shrub produces lemon-yellow flowers during mid- and late winter.
- *Viburnum* x *bodnantense*: hardy deciduous shrub with sweetly scented, rose-tinted white flowers from early to late winter. 'Dawn' has richly fragrant flowers.
- *Viburnum farreri*: hardy deciduous shrub with richly scented white flowers, tinged pink, from early to late winter – and often into early spring.

Spring-flowering shrubs & trees

Are there many to choose from?

As the year progresses, there is an increasing number of shrubs and trees bursting into colour and brightening gardens. Some shrubs and trees are known solely for their spring flowers, while others start in spring and continue into early summer. The starting and ending of spring – as well as other seasons – is increasingly unsure, but this does not spoil the beauty and seasonal inspiration of spring-flowering shrubs and trees. Additionally, some have fragrant flowers.

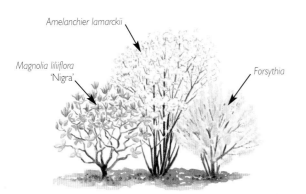

Amelanchier lamarckii

Magnolia liliiflora 'Nigra'

Forsythia

This grouping of deciduous shrubs creates instant eye appeal early in the season with its varied and richly coloured flowers.

RUSTIC SPRING FLOWERS

The popular and rural evergreen shrub *Ulex europaeus* 'Flore Pleno' (Double-flowered Gorse) is spiny, and has honey-scented, golden-yellow flowers mainly from early to late spring but often intermittently through to late winter of the following year. It is ideal for country gardens and superb when planted close to a rustic fence, such as a post-and-rail type. It is a shrub steeped in superstition, and it is said that if a horse eats the spiny branches it encourages the animal to develop further whiskers. The spiny stems also have a practical use – line seed drills (after sowing) with pieces of stem to prevent mice getting at the seeds. The plant also has a romantic association encapsulated in the saying: 'When the gorse is out of bloom, kissing's out of season.'

Amelanchier lamarckii
June Berry (UK/USA)
Shadbush (UK/USA)
Snowy Mespilus (UK)
Hardy, deciduous, large shrub or small tree with masses of pure-white, star-shaped flowers during mid-spring. In autumn the leaves assume red and soft yellow shades.

Soil and position: moisture-retentive but well-drained soil in light shade or full sun.

Pruning: no regular pruning is needed, other than cutting out damaged branches in spring after the flowers fade.

↕ 4.5–5.4 m (15–18 ft) ↔ 3.6–4.5 m (12–15 ft)

Choisya ternata
Mexican Orange Flower (UK/USA)
Slightly tender, bushy, evergreen shrub with terminal clusters of sweetly scented, orange-blossom-like white flowers, mainly during mid- and late spring; also intermittently throughout summer. The leaves, if bruised, emit a bouquet reminiscent of oranges.

Soil and position: fertile, deeply prepared, well-drained soil and a sheltered position in full sun.

Pruning: no regular pruning is needed, other than cutting out frost-damaged shoots in spring.

↕ 1.5–1.8 m (5–6 ft) ↔ 1.5–2.1 m (5–7 ft)

Forsythia x intermedia
Golden Bells (UK/USA)
Hardy, deciduous shrub that in early and mid-spring produces masses of golden-yellow flowers. The leaves appear as flowering finishes. Several superb varieties.

Soil and position: fertile, deeply prepared, moisture-retentive soil in full sun or light shade.

Pruning: regular pruning is essential; as soon as flowers fade, cut out all shoots that bore flowers to within an inch or so of the old wood.

↕ 1.8–2.5 m (6–8 ft) ↔ 1.5–2.1 m (5–7 ft)

Magnolia liliiflora 'Nigra'

Hardy, deciduous shrub with straggly growth and mid-green, oblong to pear-shaped leaves and dark, reddish-purple, chalice-shaped flowers up to 10 cm (4 in) wide in mid-spring and into early summer. At first the flowers are upright.

Soil and position: loamy, deeply prepared, well-drained but moisture-retentive soil and a sheltered position.

Pruning: no regular pruning is needed.

↕ 3 m (10 ft) ↔ 2.4 m (8 ft)

Magnolia stellata
Star Magnolia (UK/USA)

Hardy, slow-growing, deciduous shrub with a rounded but compact habit and lance-shaped, mid-green leaves up to 10 cm (4 in) long. During early and mid-spring it develops fragrant, star-shaped, white flowers up to 10 cm (4 in) wide. There are several superb forms, including 'Waterlily' with large, petal-packed flowers.

Soil and position: deeply prepared, well-drained but moisture-retentive soil and a sheltered position.

Pruning: no regular pruning is needed.

↕ 2.4–3 m (8–10 ft) ↔ 2.4–3 m (8–10 ft)

Prunus 'Accolade'

Hardy, deciduous, open and graceful ornamental cherry tree with clusters of blush-pink, semi-double flowers during early and mid-spring. When at the bud stage, the flowers are deep rosy-pink.

Soil and position: well-drained but moisture-retentive, slightly chalky soil and a wind-sheltered position.

Pruning: no regular pruning is needed. However, if shaping is needed, tackle this in early summer when the tree's sap is starting to rise.

↕ 4.5–6 m (15–20 ft) ↔ 4.5–7.6 m (15–25 ft)

Rhododendron luteum

Also known as *Rhododendron flavum* and *Azalea luteum*, this hardy, deciduous shrub creates masses of fragrant, rich yellow, funnel-shaped flowers during late spring and into early summer. In autumn, the leaves assume rich shades of purple, crimson and orange.

Soil and position: fertile, moisture-retentive, slightly acid, light soil and a position in dappled light.

Pruning: no regular pruning is needed, other than cutting out frosted stems when the flowers fade.

↕ 1.8–3 m (6–10 ft) ↔ 1.5–2.1 m (5–7 ft)

Spiraea 'Arguta'
Bridal Wreath (UK)
Foam of May (UK)

Hardy, somewhat twiggy, dense, deciduous shrub with masses of pure white flowers during mid- and late spring. The mid-green leaves form an attractive foil for the flowers.

Soil and position: fertile, deeply prepared, moisture-retentive but well-drained soil and a position in full sun.

Pruning: no regular pruning is needed, other than trimming back long shoots in mid-summer.

↕ 1.8–2.4 m (6–8 ft) ↔ 1.5–2.1 m (5–7 ft)

OTHERS TO CONSIDER

- *Berberis darwinii* (**Darwin's Berberis**): hardy, evergreen shrub that produces rich yellow flowers during late spring.
- *Berberis* x *stenophylla*: hardy, evergreen shrub with golden-yellow flowers during mid-spring.
- *Chaenomeles speciosa* (**Japanese Quince**): hardy, deciduous shrub with flowers in shades of red from late winter into spring. Several varieties, in colours including rose-pink, crimson-red and orange-red – as well as white.
- *Malus* x *purpurea* 'Lemoinei': hardy, deciduous tree with single, purple-crimson flowers during mid- and late spring.
- *Prunus padus* (**Bird Cherry**): hardy, deciduous tree with long tassels of almond-scented white flowers during late spring. The form 'Grandiflora' has longer flower tassels.
- *Prunus subhirtella* 'Pendula' (**Weeping Spring Cherry**): hardy, spreading and weeping deciduous tree with pinkish-white flowers.

Summer-flowering shrubs & trees

There are summer-flowering shrubs and trees for all gardens, whatever their size. Some shrubs are low and ideal for small gardens, while others are more dominant and better for larger areas. Some summer-flowering shrubs have massed flowers, perhaps yellow and dominant when positioned in strong light. The range of colours is wide and encompasses white through to blue and red. Whatever your preference, there are shrubs and trees to please you.

How wide is the range?

FRAGRANT SUMMERS

If rich, heady, late summer fragrances tend to delight you, you should plant one of the many varieties of *Buddleja davidii* (Butterfly Bush) that are available. During mid- and late summer – and often even into early autumn – it will produce plume-like clusters of fragrant flowers, in a range of colours including blue, white, lilac and violet-purple.

For a late spring and early summer display, *Syringa vulgaris* (Common Lilac) and its many varieties will not disappoint you. There are single, semi-double and double-flowered forms, in colours including white, mauve, lavender-blue, soft pink and deep purple.

For a late-summer display, try this grouping of bright-flowered shrubs. The colours blue, white and yellow will always create an attractive, distinctive and harmonizing feature in the garden.

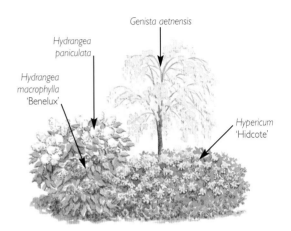

Genista aetnensis

Hydrangea paniculata

Hydrangea macrophylla 'Benelux'

Hypericum 'Hidcote'

Buddleja alternifolia
Also known as *Buddleia alternifolia*, this hardy, deciduous shrub has arching and cascading stems that from early to mid-summer become drenched in sweetly scented, lavender-blue flowers.

Soil and position: deeply prepared, friable, well-drained but moisture-retentive soil in full sun. It grows well in slightly chalky soils.

Pruning: immediately the flowers fade, cut back stems by two-thirds. This helps to create a neatly shaped shrub.

↕ 3–4.5 m (10–15 ft)   ↔ 3–4.5 m (10–15 ft)

Caryopteris x clandonensis
Bluebeard (UK/USA)
Relatively hardy, bushy, deciduous shrub with aromatic grey-green leaves. During late summer and into autumn it bears clusters of blue flowers. There are several varieties, including 'Arthur Simmonds' (bright blue), 'Heavenly Blue' (deep blue) and 'Kew Blue' (rich blue).

Soil and position: well-drained soil and a sunny, wind-protected position.

Pruning: in spring, cut back the previous year's shoots to young and healthy buds. Remove weak stems completely.

↕ 60 cm–1.2 m (2–4 ft)   ↔ 60–90 cm (2–3 ft)

Ceanothus x delileanus 'Gloire de Versailles'
Also known as *Ceanothus* 'Gloire de Versailles', this hardy, deciduous shrub has a lax nature and from mid- to late summer – and often into early autumn – bears long clusters of fragrant, soft powder-blue flowers.

Soil and position: moderately fertile, light and friable, deeply prepared, moisture-retentive soil and full sun.

Pruning: in spring of each year, cut back the previous year's shoots to within 7.5 cm (3 in) of the old wood.

↕ 1.8–2.4 m (6–8 ft)   ↔ 1.8–2.4 m (6–8 ft)

Ceratostigma willmottianum

Chinese Plumbago (USA)
Hardy Plumbago (UK)

Half-hardy, deciduous shrub with diamond-shaped leaves that in autumn assume rich red shades. In mid- and late summer it bears small, rich blue flowers.

Soil and position: fertile, well-drained but moisture-retentive soil and a sunny position sheltered from cold wind.

Pruning: prune yearly, in early spring; cut back old shoots to within a few inches of the ground.

⬆ 60–90 cm (2–3 ft) ↔ 60–90 cm (2–3 ft)

Cistus x *dansereaui*

Rock Rose (UK/USA)
Sun Rose (UK)

Also known as *Cistus* x *lusitanicus*, this evergreen shrub has lance-shaped, dark green leaves and white, 5 cm (2 in) wide, flowers splashed with crimson during early and mid-summer.

Soil and position: light, well-drained, rather poor soil and a position in full sun. Shelter from cold wind is essential.

Pruning: no regular pruning is needed, other than cutting out dead, straggly and winter-damaged shoots in spring.

⬆ 30–60 cm (1–2 ft) ↔ 45–60 cm (1½–2 ft)

Corokia cotoneaster

Wire-netting Bush (UK)

Unusual and distinctive, slightly tender evergreen shrub with masses of stiff, intertwined shoots that resemble wire-netting. During early summer it produces bright yellow, star-like flowers. These are followed by round, red fruits.

Soil and position: light, well-drained, moderately poor soil in full sun and with shelter from cold wind.

Pruning: no regular pruning is needed, other than occasionally thinning out congested plants.

⬆ 1.5–1.8 m (5–6 ft) ↔ 1.5–1.8 m (5–6 ft)

Eucryphia x *nymansensis*

Slightly tender, vigorous, evergreen shrubby tree with shiny green leaves and distinctive, creamy flowers about 6.5 cm (2¾ in) wide during late summer and into early autumn. They are borne singly or in small clusters.

Soil and position: neutral to slightly acid, moisture-retentive soil in full sun or light shade. It needs protection from cold winds.

Pruning: no regular pruning is needed, other than cutting out the growing tips of young plants to encourage bushiness.

⬆ 2.4–5.4 m (8–15 ft) ↔ 1.8–2.4 m (6–8 ft)

Genista aetnensis

Mt Etna Broom (UK/USA)

Large, deciduous shrub with a lax and informal nature and light green, rush-like branches bearing a few mid-green leaves. In mid- and late summer it produces clusters of golden-yellow flowers.

Soil and position: light, well-drained soil and full sun are needed. It dislikes root disturbance, so always buy container-grown plants.

Pruning: no regular pruning is needed, other than cutting out damaged shoots in spring.

⬆ 4.5–6 m (15–20 ft) ↔ 4.5–5.4 m (15–18 ft)

Genista cinerea

Hardy, deciduous, elegant large shrub with slender stems and small, grey-green leaves. The arching stems bear sweetly scented, yellow flowers in clusters up to 7.5 cm (3 in) long during early and mid-summer.

Soil and position: light, poor, well-drained soil suits it best, and in full sun. Always buy container-grown plants as it dislikes soil disturbance.

Pruning: no regular pruning is needed, other than cutting out winter-damaged shoots in spring.

⬆ 2.4–3 m (8–10 ft) ↔ 1.8–2.4 m (6–8 ft)

Genista hispanica

Spanish Broom (USA)
Spanish Gorse (UK)

Hardy, deciduous shrub with a dense nature, spiny stems and clusters of deep yellow flowers during early and mid-summer. When in flower it creates an eye-catching feature.

Soil and position: light, slightly poor, well-drained soil and a sheltered position in full sun.

Pruning: no regular pruning is needed. Nip out the growing tips of young plants to encourage bushiness.

↕ 60–90 cm (2–3 ft)　↔ 1.5–2.4 m (5–8 ft)

Hebe 'Autumn Glory'

Shrubby Veronica (UK)

Hardy evergreen with glossy-green leaves, edged in red when young, and deep purplish-blue flowers from mid-summer to autumn. 'Midsummer Beauty' has lavender-purple flowers.

Soil and position: well-drained soil – from slightly chalky to slightly acid – and full sun. It grows well in coastal areas.

Pruning: no regular pruning is needed, other than cutting back sparse and leggy plants in spring.

↕ 60–75 cm (2–2½ ft)　↔ 60–75 cm (2–2½ ft)

Helichrysum italicum

Curry Plant (UK)
White-leaf Everlasting (USA)

Also known as *Helichrysum angustifolium* and *Helichrysum serotinum*, it is an evergreen shrub with narrow, silvery-grey, needle-like leaves that reveal a bouquet reminiscent of curry. Throughout much of summer it displays clusters of mustard-yellow flowers.

Soil and position: light, moderately poor, well-drained soil in full sun. Avoid wet and cold soils.

Pruning: no regular pruning is needed, other than cutting back old, straggly shoots in spring, as well as those damaged by winter frosts.

↕ 30–38 cm (12–15 in)　↔ 38–60 cm (15–24 in)

Hibiscus syriacus

Shrubby Mallow (UK)

Hardy, deciduous, bushy shrub with an upright stance and three-lobed, rich-green leaves. From mid-summer to autumn it bears 7.5 cm (3 in) wide flowers in a range of colours, including violet-blue, white with red centres, and rose-pink.

Soil and position: fertile, well-drained but moisture-retentive soil in a warm, wind-sheltered position.

Pruning: no regular pruning is needed, other than shortening long shoots immediately flowering finishes. Also, in spring cut out frost-damaged shoot tips.

↕ 1.8–3 m (6–10 ft)　↔ 1.2–1.8 m (4–6 ft)

Hydrangea arborescens

Hills of Snow (USA)

Hardy, deciduous shrub with large, mop-like heads tightly packed with dull white flowers during mid- and late summer – and sometimes into early autumn. The form 'Grandiflora' has larger, pure white flowerheads.

Soil and position: fertile, moisture-retentive soil and a position in full sun or light shade.

Pruning: regular pruning is essential. In late winter or early spring, cut back by half the shoots that flowered during the previous year.

↕ 1.2–1.8 m (4–6 ft)　↔ 1.2–1.8 m (4–6 ft)

Hydrangea macrophylla

Common Hydrangea (UK)
French Hydrangea (USA)

Hardy, deciduous, rounded shrub with light green leaves. There are two types: Hortensias have mop-like flowerheads, 13–20 cm (5–8 in) wide (illustrated), while Lacecaps reveal flat heads, 10–15 cm (4–6 in) across. Flowers from mid-summer to early autumn.

Soil and position: fertile, slightly acid, moisture-retentive soil in dappled light.

Pruning: little pruning is needed, other than cutting out 2–3-year-old shoots at ground level in spring.

↕ 1.2–1.8 m (4–6 ft)　↔ 1.2–1.8 m (4–6 ft)

Hydrangea paniculata

Hardy, deciduous shrub with long stems bearing large, pyramidal heads, up to 20 cm (8 in) long, of white flowers during late summer and early autumn. The form 'Grandiflora' bears flowerheads up to 45 cm (18 in) long.

Soil and position: fertile, moisture-retentive soil and full sun or light shade.

Pruning: regular pruning is essential. In late winter or early spring, cut back by half shoots that flowered during the previous year.

↕ 2.4–3 m (8–10 ft) ↔ 2.4–3 m (8–10 ft)

Hypericum 'Hidcote'

Rose of Sharon (UK/USA)
St John's Wort (UK)

Hardy, semi-evergreen, bushy shrub with dark green leaves. From mid-summer to autumn it bears 7.5 cm (3 in) wide, saucer-shaped, waxy, golden-yellow flowers.

Soil and position: fertile, moisture-retentive but well-drained soil and full sun. Avoid positions in shade as this reduces the shrub's ability to flower.

Pruning: little pruning is needed. However, in spring cut back extra long shoots to their base.

↕ 90 cm–1.5 m (3–5 ft) ↔ 1.5–2.1m (5–7 ft)

Kalmia latifolia

Calico Bush (UK/USA)
Mountain Laurel (UK/USA)

Hardy, evergreen shrub with lance-shaped, glossy, mid-green leaves and pale blue to rosy-red, saucer-shaped flowers borne in rounded clusters up to 10 cm (4 in) wide during early summer.

Soil and position: light, moisture-retentive, lime-free soil and partial shade. Moist, cool soil is essential – mulch the soil in spring.

Pruning: no regular pruning is needed, other than removing old flowerheads.

↕ 1.8–3 m (6–10 ft) ↔ 1.8–2.4 m (6–8 ft)

Kolkwitzia amabilis

Beauty Bush (UK/USA)

Hardy, deciduous shrub with arching branches bearing oval, dark green leaves. During early summer it bears foxglove-like pink flowers with yellow throats. The stems have peeling, brown bark.

Soil and position: well-drained but moisture-retentive soil in full sun or light shade.

Pruning: regular pruning is essential to encourage the regular production of flowers. As soon as flowers fade, cut out some of the older shoots.

↕ 1.8–3 m (6–10 ft) ↔ 1.5–2.4 m (5–8 ft)

Laburnum x watereri 'Vossii'

Golden Chain Tree (UK/USA)
Golden Rain Tree (UK)

Hardy, deciduous trees with distinctive, pendulous clusters, up to 60 cm (2 ft) long, of fragrant, golden-yellow flowers in early summer. The seeds and pods are poisonous; do not plant near children's play areas or ponds.

Soil and position: moisture-retentive but well-drained soil either in full sun or light shade.

Pruning: no regular pruning is needed, other than shaping when young.

↕ 3–4.5 m (10–15 ft) ↔ 3–3.6 m (10–12 ft)

Magnolia sieboldii

Hardy, deciduous shrub or small tree with dark green leaves and white, bowl-shaped, fragrant flowers, 7.5 cm (3 in) wide, from early to late summer. They have conspicuous rosy-crimson or maroon stamens at their centres. Only a few flowers appear at one time.

Soil and position: well-drained, moderately fertile soil and sheltered from strong, cold winds.

Pruning: no regular pruning is needed, other than cutting out winter-damaged branches in spring.

↕ 3–4.5 m (10–15 ft) ↔ 3–3.6 m (10–12 ft)

Olearia x *haastii*

Daisy Bush (UK/USA)
Tree Aster (USA)

Hardy, evergreen shrub with glossy leaves; their undersides are grey-white. During mid- and late summer it bears terminal clusters of densely packed, white, daisy-like flowers.

Soil and position: well-drained but moisture-retentive soil in a sunny, wind-sheltered position.

Pruning: no regular pruning is needed, other than cutting out any dead shoots in spring.

⬆ 1.8–2.1 m (6–7 ft) ↔ 2.1–2.7 m (7–9 ft)

Paeonia rockii

Also known as *Paeonia suffruticosa* 'Rock's Variety', or *Paeonia suffruticosa rockii*, this slightly tender deciduous shrub develops large, white flowers, richly and prominently blotched in maroon-crimson during early summer.

Soil and position: moderately fertile, moisture-retentive yet well-drained soil in full sun or light shade.

Pruning: no regular pruning is needed, except to cut off dead shoots in spring.

⬆ 1.5–1.8 m (5–6 ft) ↔ 1.5–1.8 m (5–6 ft)

Philadelphus hybrids

Mock Orange (UK/USA)

Hardy, deciduous shrubs with lax natures and single or double, sweetly fragrant, white, cup-shaped flowers during early and mid-summer. There are many hybrids, in a range of sizes.

Soil and position: Moderately fertile, well-drained yet moisture-retentive soil in full sun or partial shade.

Pruning: After the flowers fade, thin out old wood; retain young shoots.

⬆ 90 cm–3 m (3–10 ft) ↔ 90 cm–3 m (3–10 ft)

Potentilla fruticosa

Shrubby Cinquefoil (UK/USA)

Hardy, deciduous, bushy but compact shrub with masses of buttercup-yellow, 2.5 cm (1 in) wide, flowers from early to late summer – and sometimes into autumn. There are several superb hybrids, in colours including soft yellow, glowing red and tangerine-red.

Soil and position: light, moisture-retentive but well-drained soil in full sun.

Pruning: no regular pruning is needed, other than clipping of dead flowerheads.

⬆ 1–1.2 m (3½–4 ft) ↔ 1–1.2 m (3½–4 ft)

Romneya coulteri var. *trichocalyx*

Californian Tree Poppy (UK)
Tree Poppy (UK)

Hardy, semi-woody shrub with herbaceous-like stems that bear blue-green leaves and slightly fragrant, poppy-like, white flowers up to 13 cm (5 in) wide from mid- to late summer – and sometimes into early autumn.

Soil and position: light, deeply prepared, fertile, moisture-retentive but well-drained soil in full sun.

Pruning: every autumn, cut stems down to within a few centimetres of the soil.

⬆ 90 cm–1.2 m (3–4 ft) ↔ 90 cm (3 ft)

Syringa meyeri

Hardy, deciduous, small-leaved lilac with violet-purple flowers borne in small, rounded clusters up to 10 cm (4 in) long during early summer. Occasionally, there is a further flush of flowers.

Soil and position: fertile, deeply prepared, well-drained but moisture-retentive soil in full sun or light shade.

Pruning: no regular pruning is needed, other than cutting out any dead shoots in spring.

⬆ 1.5–1.8 m (5–6 ft) ↔ 1.2–1.5 m (4–5 ft)

Syringa vulgaris
Common Lilac (UK/USA)

Hardy, deciduous shrub or small tree with fragrant flowers borne in large, erect pyramids during late spring and early summer. There are single, semi-double and double varieties, in colours including white, mauve, lavender-blue, soft pink and deep purple.

Soil and position: fertile, deeply prepared, well-drained but moisture-retentive soil in full sun or light shade.

Pruning: no regular pruning is needed, other than cutting out any dead shoots in spring.

⬆ 2.4–3.6 m (8–12 ft) ↔ 1.8–3 m (6–10 ft)

Viburnum opulus 'Roseum'
Snowball Bush (UK/USA)

Also known as *Viburnum opulus* 'Sterile', this deciduous, bushy shrub has white flowers, initially green, borne in large, dominant, round, flowerheads during early summer.

Soil and position: deeply prepared, moderately fertile, moisture-retentive soil and a warm, sheltered position.

Pruning: no regular pruning is needed, other than cutting out dead wood as soon as the flowers fade. Also, thin out congested stems.

⬆ 2.4–3.6 m (8–12 ft) ↔ 2.4–3.6 m (8–12 ft)

Weigela hybrids

Hardy, deciduous, wide-spreading shrub with arching branches bearing masses of flowers during early summer. There are many varieties, including 'Abel Carrière' (soft rose), 'Bristol Ruby' (ruby-red) and 'Newport Red' (bright red).

Soil and position: fertile, deeply prepared, well-drained but moisture-retentive soil in full sun or light shade.

Pruning: regular pruning is essential. As soon as the flowers fade, cut back all flowered shoots to within a few centimetres of the old wood.

⬆ 1.5–1.8 m (5–6 ft) ↔ 1.5–2.4 m (5–8 ft)

OTHERS TO CONSIDER

- *Buddleja davidii* (**Butterfly Bush/Orange-eye Buddleia/Summer Lilac**): hardy, deciduous shrub with large, plume-like, terminal heads of fragrant flowers during mid- and late summer – and into autumn. Many colours, including violet-purple, blue, white and lilac.
- *Buddleja fallowiana* '**Alba**': half-hardy, bushy, deciduous shrub with sweetly scented creamy-white flowers in long, terminal clusters from mid-summer to early autumn. It is hardier than the species, which has lavender flowers.
- *Buddleja globosa* (**Orange-ball Tree**): evergreen, or semi-evergreen in cold areas, shrub with fragrant, rounded, orange-yellow flowers during early summer.
- *Carpenteria californica*: bushy, almost evergreen shrub often grown in the shelter of a wall. The rich, glossy-green leaves are a foil for the large, fragrant, single, anemone-shaped white flowers that appear in early and mid-summer.
- *Cercis siliquastrum* (**Judas Tree/Love Tree**): hardy, deciduous tree or large shrub with pea-shaped, rose-purple flowers borne on naked branches in early summer.
- *Cornus florida* f. *rubra* (**Flowering Dogwood**): hardy, deciduous shrub or small tree with pink and white, petal-like bracts (modified leaves) during late spring and early summer. Also, coloured autumn leaves.
- *Cytisus* x *beanii* (**Broom**): hardy, dwarf, deciduous and semi-prostrate shrub with deep golden-yellow flowers during late spring and early summer.
- *Cytisus* x *praecox* (**Warminster Broom**): hardy, deciduous shrub with creamy-white, pea-shaped flowers during late spring and early summer.
- *Davidia involucrata* (**Dove Tree/Handkerchief Tree**): hardy, deciduous tree with large, creamy-white bracts (modified leaves) during early summer.
- *Deutzia* '**Magicien**': hardy, deciduous shrub with lance-shaped, pale to mid-green leaves and large, mauve-pink flowers with white during early and mid-summer. The flowers are borne in rounded clusters.
- *Fuchsia magellanica* (**Lady's Eardrops**): slightly tender, bushy shrub with crimson and purple pendent flowers from mid-summer to autumn.
- *Indigofera heterantha*: also known as *Indigofera gerardiana*, this slightly tender deciduous shrub is often grown in the shelter of a wall. Clusters of rose-purple flowers appear from mid-summer to autumn. The grey-green leaves have a slightly fern-like appearance.
- *Kerria japonica* '**Pleniflora**' (**Bachelor's Buttons/Japanese Rose**): hardy, deciduous shrub with double, orange-yellow flowers during late spring and early summer.
- *Leycesteria formosa*: hardy, deciduous shrub with heart-shaped, mid-green leaves and white, funnel-shaped flowers with claret-bracts during mid- and late summer. These are followed in mid-autumn by round, purple-black fruits.
- *Spartium junceum* (**Spanish Broom/Weaver's Broom**): hardy, deciduous shrub with rush-like stems and fragrant, golden-yellow flowers from early to late summer.

Autumn-coloured shrubs & trees

When are the best colours seen?

Many deciduous shrubs and trees have leaves that in autumn assume rich colours before falling. During some seasons, leaf colours are better than others – in dry and cold years the colours will be much richer and brighter than in years when the weather is wet and continually damp and misty. Strong autumn winds will also quickly strip shrubs and trees of their leaves. Do not forget to rake up all the fallen leaves and add them to a compost heap.

AUTUMN-COLOURED HEDGE

The popular deciduous tree *Fagus sylvatica*, widely known as the Common Beech and European Beech, is frequently planted as a hedge. The broadly oval, mid-green leaves, bright green when young and newly emerging, assume rich yellow and russet tones in autumn. As a hedge, it grows 2.4–3.6 m (8–12 ft) high and 1–1.5 m (3½–5 ft) wide. It is an ideal hedge for filtering cold wind along a boundary, has a slow-growing nature and needs trimming in mid-summer.

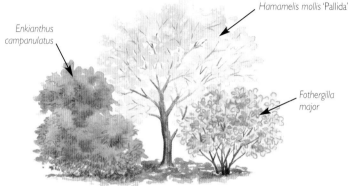

Enkianthus campanulatus

Hamamelis mollis 'Pallida'

Fothergilla major

In autumn, the leaves of many shrubs and trees become attractively coloured, which is a considerable bonus, since most also have attractive flowers.

Cercidiphyllum japonicum
Katsura Tree (UK/USA)

Hardy, deciduous tree with rounded and somewhat heart-shaped leaves. When unfolding in spring they are red, later rich green and with red and yellow tints in autumn. On still autumn days the tree has the aroma of burnt sugar.

Soil and position: moderately fertile, slightly acid, moisture-retentive soil and shelter from cold winds and early-morning frost. A light overhead canopy from deciduous trees is ideal.

Pruning: no pruning is needed.

↑ 6–7.5 m (20–25 ft) ↔ 4.5–6 m (15–20 ft)

Cornus florida
Flowering Dogwood (UK/USA)

Hardy, deciduous shrub or tree with dark green leaves that in autumn assume brilliant shades of scarlet and orange. Additionally, in late spring and early summer it bears green flowers surrounded by white, petal-like bracts (modified leaves).

Soil and position: light, deeply prepared, neutral or slightly acid, well-drained but moisture-retentive soil and full sun.

Pruning: no regular pruning is needed.

↑ 3–4.5 m (10–15 ft) ↔ 3–5.4 m (10–18 ft)

Enkianthus campanulatus

Hardy, deciduous tree with dull green, finely tooth-edged leaves that in autumn turn brilliant red. Additionally, in late spring and early summer it displays creamy-white, bell-shaped flowers with red veins.

Soil and position: neutral to slightly acid, woodland-type soil that does not dry out, and a position in sun and with shelter from cold winds.

Pruning: no regular pruning is needed.

↑ 1.8–2.7 m (6–9 ft) ↔ 1.2–1.8 m (4–6 ft)

Fothergilla major
Hardy, deciduous, slow-growing shrub with dark green leaves which in autumn assume rich red and orange-yellow tints. In late spring, before the leaves appear, it bears white, sweetly scented, bottle-brush-like flowerheads.

Soil and position: moderately fertile, moisture-retentive peaty soil in full sun.

Pruning: no regular pruning is needed. Where shoots are damaged during winter, these can be cut out in spring.

↕ 1.8–2.4 m (6–8 ft) ↔ 1.5–1.8 m (5–6 ft)

Hamamelis mollis 'Pallida'
Chinese Witch Hazel (UK/USA)

Hardy, deciduous shrub with slightly pear-shaped, mid-green leaves that in autumn assume rich yellow tints. During mid- and late winter it reveals spider-like, sulphur-yellow flowers.

Soil and position: neutral or slightly acid, moisture-retentive but well-drained soil. A sunny or lightly shaded position, sheltered from cold wind, suits it.

Pruning: no regular pruning is needed, other than cutting out any dead wood in spring.

↕ 1.8–3 m (6–10 ft) ↔ 2.1–3 m (7–10 ft)

Liquidambar styraciflua
American Sweet Gum (USA)
Red Gum (USA)
Sweet Gum (UK/USA)

Hardy, deciduous tree with deeply divided, five- or seven-lobed, shiny green leaves that in autumn assume rich shades of crimson, purple and orange. Eventually it forms a large tree.

Soil and position: well-drained but moisture-retentive soil in full sun or partial shade.

Pruning: no regular pruning is needed, other than cutting out dead or crossing branches in early winter.

↕ 5.4–7.5 m (18–25 ft) ↔ 2.4–3.6 m (8–12 ft)

Parrotia persica
Hardy, deciduous, slow-growing tree or large shrub with oval to pear-shaped, mid-green leaves that in autumn assume shades of gold, amber and crimson. Eventually it forms a large tree.

Soil and position: fertile, well-drained but moisture-retentive soil in light shade or full sun. Slightly acid soil is best, although it does tolerate lime.

Pruning: no regular pruning is needed.

↕ 3–5.4 m (10–18 ft) ↔ 3–4.5 m (10–15 ft)

Rhus typhina
Stag's Horn Sumach (UK/USA)
Velvet Sumach (USA)

Hardy, deciduous shrub with leaves formed of 13–26 mid-green leaflets which in autumn assume rich shades of orange, red and purple. The stems are covered with reddish hairs.

Soil and position: well-drained but moisture-retentive soil in full sun.

Pruning: none is needed when it is grown for autumn colour.

↕ 2.4–3.6 m (8–12 ft) ↔ 2.4–3.6 m (8–12 ft)

OTHERS TO CONSIDER

- *Acer palmatum* (Japanese Maple): hardy, deciduous, slow-growing tree with five- or seven-lobed leaves that in autumn assume rich colours.
- *Berberis thunbergii* (Japanese Barberry): hardy, rounded and compact deciduous shrub with small, pear-shaped, pale to mid-green leaves that turn brilliant red.
- *Fagus sylvatica* (Common Beech/European Beech): large, deciduous, hardy tree (that is sometimes planted as a hedge) with mid-green leaves that assume rich yellow and russet tones in autumn.
- *Ginkgo biloba* (Maidenhair Tree): hardy, deciduous conifer with pale green leaves which in autumn become soft golden-yellow.
- *Liriodendron tulipifera* (Tulip Tree): distinctive leaves, with an almost square central lobe, that turn butter-yellow in autumn.
- *Taxodium distichum* (Bald Cypress/Swamp Cypress): hardy, deciduous conifer with yellow-green leaves, rich brown in autumn.

Coloured bark and stems

Is special pruning required?

Trees with coloured bark need very little attention – apart from occasionally trimming off a branch, pruning is not a consideration. However, shrubs and trees grown for their coloured stems – such as the Dogwoods *Cornus sericea* (also known as *Cornus stolonifera*) and *Cornus alba*, as well as several forms of *Salix alba* (White Willow) – need annual pruning in spring in order to ensure the development of young shoots that will produce colour in the following winter.

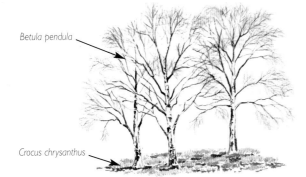

Betula pendula

Crocus chrysanthus

The bark colour of these Betula pendula *(Silver Birch) trees is enhanced by the low rays of the sun in spring.*

SINGLE OR GROUPED?

Betula pendula (Silver Birch) is a popular birch, with silvery, somewhat warty bark. Its delicate appearance makes it ideal for planting in a small group (see left). Several other types of Birch have stronger-coloured bark, however, and these trees tend to look better when grown on their own in a lawn, or in a bed or border, surrounded by a selection of low-growing shrubs.

Shrubs such as *Cornus* (Dogwoods) that are grown for their coloured winter bark are perfect for planting in large groups alongside a stream or a large, informal pond (but where damage cannot be caused to a pool liner by their roots). The mass of coloured stems, when reflected in the water and highlighted by low sunlight, invariably create a particularly memorable feature.

Acer griseum
Paperbark Maple (UK/USA)

Hardy, deciduous tree with a slow-growing nature and buff-coloured bark that peels to reveal orange-brown underbark. Additionally, the mid-green leaves assume rich scarlet and deep red shades in autumn.

Soil and position: neutral or slightly chalky, well-drained but moisture-retentive soil in full sun or light shade.

Pruning: no regular pruning is needed, except to cut out crossing and misplaced branches in spring.

↕ 3.6–4.5 m (12–15 ft) ↔ 2.4–3 m (8–10 ft)

Acer pensylvanicum
Moosewood (UK/USA)
Snakebark Maple (UK/USA)

Hardy, deciduous tree with trunk and branches striped with jagged white lines. The young wood is green, then reddish-brown and later striped. The pale to mid-green leaves have three tapering lobes and in autumn assume soft yellow shades.

Soil and position: well-drained but moisture-retentive soil in full sun or partial shade.

Pruning: no regular pruning is needed.

↕ 5.4–7.5 m (18–25 ft) ↔ 3–4.5 m (10–15 ft)

Arbutus x andrachnoides
Also known as *Arbutus hybrida*, this mostly hardy, evergreen tree has cinnamon-red bark that glows when in direct sunlight. The leaves are dark green and leathery, while in spring it has ivory-white, pitcher-shaped, nodding flowers.

Soil and position: slightly acid or neutral, moisture-retentive but well-drained soil in full sun or dappled shade and shelter from cold wind, especially when young.

Pruning: no regular pruning is needed.

↕ 3–4.5 m (10–15 ft) ↔ 2.1–2.7 m (7–9 ft)

Betula utilis var. jacquemontii

Also known as *Betula jacquemontii*, this hardy, deciduous tree has a dazzling white trunk and branches. Some forms of this magnificent tree have pinkish-brown and ochre-cream bark.

Soil and position: well-drained, deeply prepared, slightly acid soil in full sun or light shade.

Pruning: no regular pruning is needed, other than occasionally cutting out a misplaced or damaged branch in spring.

↕ 6–9 m (20–30 ft) ↔ 3–4.5 m (10–15 ft)

Cornus sericea 'Flaviramea'

Dogwood (UK/USA)

Also known as *Cornus stolonifera* 'Flaviramea', this hardy, deciduous, vigorous, suckering shrub has a spreading nature and dark green leaves. When severely pruned annually, masses of bright greenish-yellow stems can be produced for winter colour.

Soil and position: fertile, moisture-retentive soil in full sun or partial shade.

Pruning: in mid-spring, cut back all shoots to 5–7.5 cm (2–3 in) above soil level.

↕ 1.8–2.4 m (6–8 ft) ↔ 2.1–3 m (7–10 ft)

Eucalyptus pauciflora

Cabbage Gum (UK/USA)
Ghost Gum (UK/USA)

Hardy, evergreen tree with attractive, pattern-changing bark. When first exposed, the bark is white, then darkening in an irregular pattern to grey. Adult leaves are leathery, bright glossy-green and sickle-shaped, whereas young leaves are oval to circular.

Soil and position: fertile, moisture-retentive (especially during summer) but well-drained soil – it tolerates slight chalkiness – and full sun.

Pruning: usually, little pruning is needed.

↕ 7.5–10.5 m (25–35 ft) ↔ 4.5–6 m (15–20 ft)

Prunus serrula

Birch-bark tree (UK)

Hardy, deciduous tree with spectacular bright reddish-brown, mahogany-like, peeling bark which is most noticeable on young trees. The leaves are narrow, slender-pointed and willow-like.

Soil and position: well-drained, slightly chalky soil, full sun and shelter from cold wind.

Pruning: no regular pruning is needed, but should a branch need to be removed tackle this in spring, when growth is commencing.

↕ 6–7.5 m (20–25 ft) ↔ 4.5–5.4 m (15–18 ft)

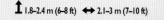

Rubus cockburnianus

Ornamental Bramble (UK/USA)

Also known as *Rubus giraldianus*, this hardy, vigorous, deciduous shrub develops upright stems with a white, waxy bloom tinged blue that are especially attractive during winter. Additionally, in early summer it bears small, purple flowers.

Soil and position: fertile, well-drained but moisture-retentive soil in full sun or partial shade.

Pruning: when the flowers fade, cut out a few old stems.

↕ 1.8–2.1 m (6–7 ft) ↔ 1.5–1.8 m (5–6 ft)

OTHERS TO CONSIDER

- *Acer davidii* (Snakebark Maple): hardy, deciduous tree with grey bark striped white. The colour is most noticeable when the tree is grown in light shade.
- *Arbutus menziesii*: hardy, evergreen tree with smooth, terracotta bark on the trunk and large branches.
- *Betula albosinensis* var. *septentrionalis*: hardy, deciduous tree mainly grown for its spectacular shiny, orange-brown bark with a grey and pink bloom.
- *Betula papyrifera* (Paper Birch): hardy, deciduous tree with white bark which, on old trees, peels off in strips.
- *Betula pendula* (Silver Birch): hardy, deciduous tree with silvery bark.
- *Cornus alba* (Dogwood): hardy, vigorous, suckering shrub with rich-red young stems in winter.
- *Cornus alba* 'Sibirica': hardy, vigorous, suckering shrub with brilliant crimson stems in winter.
- *Prunus maackii* (Amur Cherry): hardy deciduous tree with smooth, brownish-yellow, peeling bark.

Evergreen shrubs

Are evergreen shrubs fully hardy?

There are many evergreen shrubs and trees that withstand winters in temperate climates, while others, such as *Fatsia japonica* (False Castor Oil Plant), need a sunny and wind-sheltered position. Many evergreen *Elaeagnus* shrubs are fully hardy, with some having the benefit of variegated or coloured leaves. Evergreen shrubs also vary in size, from the relatively low-growing coloured-leaved Heathers (*Calluna*) to the more dominant *Elaeagnus* shrubs.

GOOD BUY SHRUBS

Evergreen shrubs are year-round, value-for-money features in a garden. Some have all-green, attractively shaped leaves, whereas others demonstrate some beautiful variegations. Most of these shrubs are long-lived, although the slightly tender *Salvia officinalis* 'Icterina' has a shorter span – nevertheless it is well worth planting. In addition, it has several close relatives, including *Salvia officinalis* 'Purpurascens' (Purple-leaved Sage), the stems and leaves of which are suffused with purple, and *Salvia officinalis* 'Tricolor', which has delightful grey-green leaves that are splashed with creamy-white and suffused with pink and purple.

This group of variegated evergreen shrubs will create colour throughout the year. Yellow-flowered Daffodils add further colour in spring.

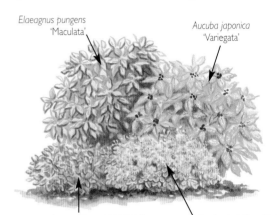

Elaeagnus pungens 'Maculata'

Aucuba japonica 'Variegata'

Euonymus fortunei 'Emerald 'n' Gold'

Brachyglottis 'Sunshine'

Aucuba japonica 'Variegata'

Gold-dust Tree (USA)
Gold-dust Plant (USA)
Spotted Laurel (UK)

Also known as *Aucuba japonica* 'Maculata', this hardy, evergreen shrub has shiny, dark green leaves spotted and splashed in yellow. It creates a colourful feature, especially in winter.

Soil and position: ordinary garden soil in full sun or partial shade.

Pruning: no regular pruning is needed, other than occasionally cutting out old stems in spring.

⬆ 3 m (10 ft) ↔ 3 m (10 ft)

Brachyglottis 'Sunshine'

Also known as *Senecio* 'Sunshine', this mound-forming evergreen shrub has silvery-grey leaves with white-felted undersides. Additionally, during early and mid-summer it bears bright yellow, daisy-like flowers.

Soil and position: deeply prepared, well-drained but moisture-retentive soil in full sun. It is ideal for planting in coastal areas.

Pruning: no regular pruning is needed, other than occasionally cutting out straggly stems in spring.

⬆ 60–1.2 m (2–4 ft) ↔ 1.2–1.5 m (4–5 ft)

Calluna vulgaris 'Gold Haze'

Heather (UK/USA)
Ling (UK/USA)
Scotch Heather (USA)

Hardy, evergreen shrub with bright, golden-yellow, scale-like leaves and white flowers during late summer and into early autumn.

Soil and position: moisture-retentive, lime-free soil and a position in full sun.

Pruning: after the flowers fade, clip them off.

⬆ 60 cm (2 ft) ↔ 60–75 cm (2–2½ ft)

Choisya ternata 'Sundance'

Mexican Orange Blossom (UK/USA)
Yellow-leaved Mexican Orange Blossom (UK)

Slightly tender, evergreen shrub with glossy, golden-yellow leaves throughout the year. Also, from late spring to early summer – and sometimes later – it bears faintly orange-blossom scented white flowers.

Soil and position: well-drained but moisture-retentive soil and a warm, wind-sheltered position.

Pruning: no regular pruning is needed, except for cutting out frost-damaged shoots in late spring.

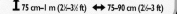 75 cm–1 m (2½–3½ ft) ↔ 75–90 cm (2½–3 ft)

Elaeagnus pungens 'Maculata'

Thorny Elaeagnus (USA)

Hardy, slow-growing, evergreen shrub with oval, leathery, glossy-green leaves that are splashed with gold. The form 'Variegata' has leaves with narrow, creamy-yellow edges.

Soil and position: moderately fertile, deeply prepared soil in full sun or light shade. Avoid shallow, chalky soil.

Pruning: no regular pruning is needed, other than cutting back long, misplaced and straggly stems in late spring. Cut out to their bases any stems that have all-green leaves.

 1.8–3 m (6–10 ft) ↔ 1.8–3 m (6–10 ft)

Euonymus fortunei 'Emerald 'n' Gold'

Hardy, dwarf and bushy evergreen shrub, densely covered with bright, golden variegated leaves that turn bronzy-pink in winter.

Soil and position: moderately fertile, ordinary garden soil in light shade or full sun encourages the best leaf colours.

Pruning: no regular pruning is needed, other than occasionally cutting out a damaged shoot in spring.

30–45 cm (1–1½ ft) ↔ 45–60 cm (1½–2 ft)

Euonymus japonicus 'Aureus'

Also known as Euonymus japonicus 'Aureopictus', this hardy, evergreen shrub has a bushy and densely branched habit with glossy, dark green leaves that are strongly marked bright yellow at their centres.

Soil and position: moderately fertile, ordinary garden soil in light shade or full sun.

Pruning: no regular pruning is needed when grown in a border, except cutting out straggly or damaged stems in spring.

1.2–1.5 m (4–5 ft) ↔ 90 cm–1.2 m (3–4 ft)

Fatsia japonica

False Castor Oil Plant (UK)
Glossy-leaved Paper Plant (USA)
Japanese Fatsia (USA)

Slightly tender, evergreen shrub with large, glossy, hand-like leaves with coarsely toothed edges. In autumn and winter it bears white flowers.

Soil and position: light, well-drained but moisture-retentive soil in a warm, wind-sheltered position.

Pruning: no pruning is necessary, except to cut out straggly and winter-damaged shoots in spring.

1.5–2.1 m (5–7 ft) ↔ 1.5–1.8 m (5–6 ft)

Ilex x altaclerensis 'Lawsoniana'

Variegated English Holly (USA)
Variegated Holly (UK)

Hardy, evergreen shrub with thick, leathery, dark green leaves heavily splashed in bright yellow. Unlike most hollies, the leaves are usually spineless.

Soil and position: deeply prepared, moisture-retentive but well-drained soil in full sun. It will rapidly lose its bright, variegated nature if positioned in shade.

Pruning: no regular pruning is needed.

3–4.5 m (10–15 ft) ↔ 2.4–3.6 m (8–12 ft)

Ilex aquifolium 'Madame Briot'

Variegated English Holly (USA)
Variegated Holly (UK)

Hardy, evergreen shrub with leathery, spiny, green leaves edged in dark yellow. Their centres are also mottled in gold and light green. The stems are purple.

Soil and position: deeply prepared, moisture-retentive but well-drained soil in full sun. It will rapidly lose its bright, variegated nature if positioned in shade.

Pruning: no regular pruning is needed.

↕ 3–5.4 m (10–18 ft) ↔ 1.8–3 m (6–10 ft)

Lonicera nitida 'Baggesen's Gold'

Golden-leaved Chinese Honeysuckle (UK)
Yellow-leaved Chinese Honeysuckle (UK)

Hardy, bushy, densely leaved evergreen shrub with small, rich golden-yellow leaves that turn yellow-green in autumn.

Soil and position: moderately fertile, moisture-retentive but well-drained soil in full sun or partial shade. The colour of the leaves is best when in full sun.

Pruning: no regular pruning is needed, other than occasionally cutting out straggly stems in spring.

↕ 1.2–1.8 m (4–6 ft) ↔ 1.2–1.5 m (4–5 ft)

Pachysandra terminalis 'Variegata'

Variegated Japanese Spurge (UK/USA)

Hardy, spreading, creeping and ground-covering evergreen shrub with deep green leaves edged in white. Small, white flowers appear during mid-spring. It is less vigorous than the all-green types.

Soil and position: poor to moderately fertile soil and a position in light shade.

Pruning: no regular pruning is needed.

↕ 25–30 cm (10–12 in) ↔ 45 cm (18 in)

Phormium tenax

New Zealand Flax (UK/USA)
New Zealand Hemp (UK/USA)

Half-hardy, distinctive, evergreen shrub with strap-like, leathery, mid- to deep green leaves. There are several forms with colourful or variegated leaves, including 'Purpureum' (bronze-purple) and 'Variegatum' (creamy-white edges).

Soil and position: moderately fertile, deeply prepared, moisture-retentive but well-drained soil in full sun.

Pruning: remove dead flower stems in early autumn.

↕ 1.5–3 m (5–10 ft) ↔ 1.2–1.5 m (4–5 ft)

Pieris japonica 'Variegata'

Slow-growing, hardy, evergreen shrub with shiny, grey-green leaves with creamy-white edges, flushed pink when young. Additionally, it bears terminal clusters of white flowers in spring.

Soil and position: lime-free, moisture-retentive soil in a sheltered position in partial shade.

Pruning: no regular pruning is needed, except removing dead flowerheads and cutting back straggly shoots as soon as the flowers fade.

↕ 1.8–2.1 m (6–7 ft) ↔ 1.8–2.1 m (6–7 ft)

Pittosporum tenuifolium

Kohuru (USA)
Tawhiwhi (USA)

Half-hardy, evergreen shrub with wavy-edged, pale-green leaves borne on almost black stems. In addition to the all-green species, there are several forms with variegated leaves. These include 'Silver Queen' (silvery-grey), 'Irene Paterson' (young leaves creamy-white) and 'Variegatum' (creamy-white edges).

Soil and position: well-drained, fertile soil. Position in full sun, sheltered from cold winds.

Pruning: during spring, shorten any straggly shoots.

↕ 1.5–3 m (5–10 ft) ↔ 1.5–2.1 m (5–7 ft)

Salvia officinalis 'Icterina'

Slightly tender, short-lived shrub that in cold regions may become semi-evergreen. Nevertheless, it is an attractive shrub, with green-and-gold variegated leaves. There are other attractive variegated forms, including 'Tricolor' (grey-green leaves splashed creamy-white).

Soil and position: light, well-drained soil in full sun and in a warm and wind-sheltered position.

Pruning: no regular pruning is needed, but in spring cut off winter-damaged and straggly shoots.

↕ 45–60 cm (1½–2 ft) ↔ 45–60 cm (1½–2 ft)

Vinca major 'Variegata'
Variegated Greater Periwinkle
(UK/USA)

Also known as *Vinca major* 'Elegantissima', this hardy, spreading and sprawling evergreen shrub has glossy, mid-green leaves edged in creamy-white. In spring and summer it has bright blue flowers.

Soil and position: well-drained soil and a bright, sunny position. Avoid excessively fertile soils and deep shade.

Pruning: no regular pruning is needed, other than cutting back long and straggly stems in summer.

↕ 15–38 cm (6–15 in) ↔ 90 cm–1.2 m (3–4 ft)

Vinca minor 'Variegata'
Variegated Lesser Periwinkle
(UK/USA)

Hardy, ground-hugging evergreen shrub with a spreading nature and glossy, dark green leaves variegated in creamy-white.

Soil and position: well-drained soil and a bright, sunny position. Avoid excessively fertile soils and deep shade.

Pruning: no regular pruning is needed, other than cutting back long and straggly stems in summer.

↕ 5–10 cm (2–4 in) ↔ 90 cm–1.2 m (3–4 ft)

Yucca filamentosa 'Variegata'

Variegated Adam's Needle (UK/USA)

Slightly tender and unusual evergreen shrub with rosettes of deep green leaves edged in whitish-yellow. Also, in mid-summer it produces plume-like heads of creamy-white, bell-shaped flowers on stems up to 1.5 m (5 ft) high.

Soil and position: light, well-drained soil in full sun, sheltered from cold wind.

Pruning: no pruning is needed.

↕ 60–75 cm (2–2½ ft) ↔ 90 cm–1.2 m (3–4 ft)

OTHERS TO CONSIDER

- *Buxus sempervirens* '**Aureovariegata**' **(Variegated Box):** also known as *Buxus sempervirens* 'Aurea Maculata', this hardy, dense and bushy evergreen shrub has glossy, dark green leaves variously splashed, striped in creamy-yellow.
- *Daphne odora* '**Aureomarginata**': rounded, evergreen shrub with narrowly lance-shaped to oval, pale green leaves with narrow creamy-white edges. It is hardier than the all-green species.
- *Elaeagnus* x *ebbingei* '**Gilt Edge**': hardy, fast-growing evergreen shrub with leathery, broadly oval, silver-grey leaves with their edges irregularly coloured golden-yellow.
- *Elaeagnus pungens* '**Dicksonii**': hardy, rounded but spreading, evergreen shrub with spiny stems. The oval, leathery, glossy-green leaves are widely and irregularly edged in golden-yellow.
- *Fatsia japonica* '**Variegata**' **(Variegated False Castor Oil Plant):** slightly tender, evergreen shrub with large, rich glossy-green leaves irregularly edged white.
- *Griselinia littoralis* '**Dixon's Cream**': frost-tender, slow-growing, evergreen shrub with thick, leathery, pear-shaped, lustrous apple-green leaves with conspicuous white variegations.
- *Hebe* x *andersonii* '**Variegata**': slightly tender, evergreen shrub with leathery, cream-and-green variegated leaves, as well as spikes of lavender flowers from mid-summer to early autumn.
- *Rhamnus alaternus* '**Argenteovariegata**' **(Variegated Buckthorn):** moderately fast-growing evergreen shrub with dark, glossy-green leaves marbled grey and with an irregular, creamy-white edging.
- *Viburnum davidii*: evergreen shrub with oval, dark green and prominently veined leaves. It also develops turquoise-blue berries.
- *Viburnum rhytidophyllum*: large, evergreen shrub with long, lance-shaped, glossy, deep green leaves, and white flowers in late spring and early summer.

Large evergreen and deciduous conifers

Can large conifers be used as focal points?

Several conifers create dominant features and are ideal for positioning towards the end of a garden and, perhaps, in a lawn. Some conifers, such as dominant yellow-leaved types like *Chamaecyparis lawsoniana* 'Lutea' and *Chamaecyparis lawsoniana* 'Winston Churchill', remain visible even into late evening. Other large conifers, such as *Calocedrus decurrens* (Incense Cedar) and *Cupressus sempervirens* (Italian Cypress) are ideal for planting in small groups.

NARROW NATURES

Several conifers are upright and narrow in habit, making them ideal for planting in a small garden. Some can be planted on their own, although *Cupressus sempervirens* (Italian Cypress) looks better in a small group. It can also introduce a Mediterranean feel. Conifers introduce permanence, so make sure they are planted in the right place and will not, after a few years, grow too large and have to be cut down.

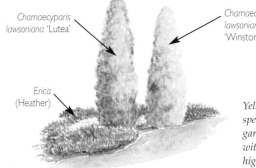

Chamaecyparis lawsoniana 'Lutea'

Chamaecyparis lawsoniana 'Winston Churchill'

Erica (Heather)

Yellow-foliaged conifers create spectacular focal points in a large garden. Surrounding the conifers with flowering Erica *(Heathers) highlights their foliage.*

Calocedrus decurrens
Californian Incense Cedar (USA)
Incense Cedar (UK)

Also known as *Libocedrus decurrens*, this hardy, slow-growing, evergreen conifer usually has a narrow, upright nature in gardens, especially when young, although with age it widens. It develops upright, dense fans of dark green leaves.

Soil and position: fertile, moisture-retentive but well-drained soil in full sun.

Pruning: no regular pruning is needed, but remember to ensure that there is only one leading shoot.

↕ 7.5–9 m (25–30 ft) ↔ 3–3.6 m (10–12 ft)

Chamaecyparis lawsoniana 'Columnaris Glauca'

Hardy, narrowly columnar, evergreen conifer that is densely packed with glaucous, pale grey foliage. It is ideal for planting in a small garden, in a group or as a focal point.

Soil and position: well-drained but moisture-retentive soil in full sun or light shade.

Pruning: no regular pruning is needed, but when young ensure there is only one leading shoot.

↕ 4.5–5.4 m (15–18 ft) ↔ 45 cm (1½ ft)

Chamaecyparis lawsoniana 'Lutea'

Hardy, evergreen, slow to moderately fast-growing conifer with a broad but columnar outline and a spire-like, slightly drooping, top. It is packed with large, flattened sprays of golden-yellow foliage. Plant it in a group or as a focal point.

Soil and position: well-drained but moisture-retentive soil in full sun.

Pruning: no regular pruning is needed, other than to ensure there is just one leading shoot.

↕ 7.5–9 m (25–30 ft) ↔ 1.8–2.1 m (6–7 ft)

Chamaecyparis lawsoniana 'Pembury Blue'

Hardy, conical, slow to moderately fast-growing evergreen conifer with sprays of silvery-blue foliage. It is often considered to be the best blue form of the Lawson Cypress. Plant it in a group of colour-contrasting conifers.

Soil and position: well-drained but moisture-retentive soil in full sun.

Pruning: no regular pruning is needed, other than to ensure that there is just one leading shoot.

⬆ 1.8–3.6 m (6–12 ft) ↔ 1–1.2 m (3½–4 ft)

Cupressus macrocarpa 'Goldcrest'

Hardy, evergreen conifer, initially with a narrow nature then broadening. It becomes drenched in rich yellow, feathery, juvenile foliage. It is sometimes used to form a hedge or screen, especially in coastal areas, but is also superb as a feature on its own.

Soil and position: well-drained but moisture-retentive soil in full sun.

Pruning: no regular pruning is needed, other than to ensure that there is just one leading shoot.

⬆ 4.5–7.5 m (15–25 ft) ↔ 1.2–1.8 m (4–6 ft)

Cupressus sempervirens

Italian Cypress (UK/USA)
Mediterranean Cypress (UK)

Distinctive, slightly tender, evergreen conifer with an upright, columnar outline. Branches are densely packed with upright, dark green foliage. It is best planted when still small and as a container-grown plant.

Soil and position: well-drained but moisture-retentive soil in full sun.

Pruning: no regular pruning is needed, other than to ensure that there is just one leading shoot.

⬆ 6–7.5 m (20–25 ft) ↔ 1.5–2.4 m (6–8 ft)

Juniperus chinensis 'Aurea'

Golden Chinese Juniper (UK)

Hardy, bushy but upright, evergreen conifer with golden-yellow, needle-like leaves in tightly packed vertical sprays. It must be positioned in full sun to produce the richest colour, and is one of the best golden, upright conifers for small gardens.

Soil and position: well-drained but moisture-retentive soil in full sun.

Pruning: no regular pruning is needed, other than to ensure that there is only one leading shoot.

⬆ 4.5–6 m (15–20 ft) ↔ 1.5 m (5 ft)

Larix decidua

European Larch (UK/USA)

Hardy, graceful, slow-growing deciduous conifer with a wind-tolerant nature. Eventually it develops into a large tree. It has bright green leaves in spring, changing to medium green and, in autumn, to golden and russet.

Soil and position: well-drained but moisture-retentive soil in full sun.

Pruning: no regular pruning is needed, other than to ensure that there is just one leading shoot.

⬆ 6–7.5 m (20–25 ft) ↔ 3.6–4 m (12–13 ft)

OTHERS TO CONSIDER

- *Chamaecyparis lawsoniana* 'Winston Churchill': hardy, evergreen conifer, eventually forming a large tree and ideal for creating a focal point at the end of a large garden. The foliage remains golden-yellow throughout the year. One of the best large, yellow-leaved Lawson Cypresses.

- *Chamaecyparis nootkatensis* 'Pendula': hardy, evergreen conifer with widely spaced branches that curve upwards towards their ends. Branchlets with dark green leaflets hang in long, graceful streamers.

- *Cunninghamia lanceolata*: hardy, evergreen, slow-growing conifer with an exotic appearance. Branches are covered with narrow, stiff, shiny, emerald-green leaves that have a centipede-like appearance.

- *Picea pungens* 'Koster': distinctive, hardy, conical, evergreen conifer with steel-blue foliage. In spring, when young shoots start to appear, it is especially attractive. It creates a dominant feature and is ideal for planting with yellow-leaved conifers.

Slow-growing and dwarf conifers

Are they suitable for rock gardens?

Many slow-growing and naturally dwarf conifers are ideal for planting in rock gardens. However, you should always be prepared to move the slow-growing types when they eventually become too large for their surroundings. They can then be planted in a garden border – perhaps around a house – or in a Heather garden where they can remain for several years. Dwarf conifers, however, can often be left in a rock garden for around 10–20 years.

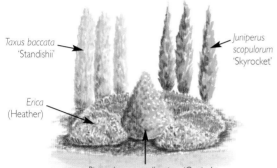

Taxus baccata 'Standishii'

Juniperus scopulorum 'Skyrocket'

Erica (Heather)

Picea glauca var. albertiana 'Conica'

Planting a range of differently shaped and coloured slow-growing conifers creates an attractive and long-term feature.

SMALL-GARDEN FEATURES

These diminutive conifers are ideal for creating colourful features in a small garden. When planted in a small island bed in a lawn, they produce colour throughout the year. Position them so that the tallest conifers are about two-thirds of the way along the length of the bed. This will help to create a feature that looks planned, rather than a medley of undisciplined plants.

To create extra colour, miniature spring-flowering bulbs look good as companions. For larger areas, where a sea of low plants is desired, *Ericas* are better. Make sure that they do not dominate, crowd out and spoil the shapes of diminutive conifers, however. All newly planted conifers should be well watered on a regular basis until they are firmly established.

Chamaecyparis lawsoniana 'Ellwood's Gold Pillar'

Hardy, evergreen, spire-like, extremely slow-growing conifer that is tightly covered with soft golden-yellow foliage. It is ideal for planting in a rock garden or scree bed, as well as in containers on a patio. It is even slower-growing than the popular *Chamaecyparis lawsoniana* 'Ellwood's Gold'.

Soil and position: well-drained but moisture-retentive soil in full sun.

Pruning: no regular pruning is needed.

↕ 75–90 cm (2½–3 ft) ↔ 25 cm (10 in)

Chamaecyparis pisifera 'Filifera Aurea'

Hardy, evergreen, slow-growing but eventually – after many years – reaches about 3 m (10 ft) high. This spectacular evergreen conifer has golden, thread-like foliage and is ideal for planting in a large rock garden, where it creates height and colour.

Soil and position: well-drained soil and a position in full sun.

Pruning: no pruning is needed.

↕ 60–90 cm (2–3 ft) ↔ 60–90 cm (2–3 ft)

Juniperus communis 'Compressa'

An exceptionally attractive, hardy, evergreen, slow-growing conifer with a compact, column-like habit and green, silvery-backed leaves that are tightly packed on upright branches. It is ideal for planting in a rock garden, scree bed or sink garden.

Soil and position: well-drained but moisture-retentive soil in full sun.

Pruning: no pruning is needed.

↕ 30–45 cm (1–1½ ft) ↔ 10–15 cm (4–6 in)

Juniperus communis 'Depressa Aurea'

Hardy, spreading, evergreen, slow-growing conifer with bright yellow foliage in spring and summer, turning bronze by autumn. Its branches and foliage have a slightly feathery nature. It is ideal for planting in a large rock garden, or alongside a path where its branches cloak the sides.

Soil and position: well-drained but moisture-retentive soil in full sun or light shade.

Pruning: no regular pruning is needed.

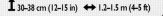
⬍ 30–38 cm (12–15 in)   ⬌ 1.2–1.5 m (4–5 ft)

Juniperus scopulorum 'Skyrocket'

Also known as *Juniperus virginiana* 'Skyrocket', this distinctive, hardy, evergreen conifer with blue-grey foliage has a narrow, columnar shape. Eventually it forms a large and distinctive feature, often 4.5 m (15 ft) or more high, but when young is ideal for planting among heathers to create height.

Soil and position: Well-drained but moisture-retentive soil in full sun.

Pruning: No pruning is needed.

⬍ 3–3.6 m (10–12 ft)   ⬌ 25–30 cm (10–12 in)

Picea glauca var. albertiana 'Conica'

Dwarf Alberta Spruce (UK)

Also known as *Picea glauca* 'Albertiana Conica', this hardy, slow-growing conifer forms a distinctive, conical outline – with age it broadens. It is densely packed with soft, grass-green foliage and is especially attractive in spring. Plant in a heather garden or large rock garden.

Soil and position: well-drained soil and a position in full sun.

Pruning: no pruning is needed.

⬍ 75–90 cm (2½–3 ft)   ⬌ 75–90 cm (2½–3 ft)

Taxus baccata 'Standishii'

Also known as *Taxus baccata* 'Fastigiata Standishii', this hardy, slow-growing, columnar, evergreen conifer has branches tightly packed with golden-yellow leaves. It is especially attractive in winter and ideal for planting amid heathers or in a large rock garden.

Soil and position: most soils, in full sun or shade.

Pruning: no pruning is needed.

⬍ 1.2–1.5 m (4–5 ft)   ⬌ 25–30 cm (10–12 in)

OTHERS TO CONSIDER

- *Abies balsamea* **'Hudsonia':** hardy, compact, dwarf, evergreen conifer. It develops a flattish top formed of grey leaves that turn mid-green in mid-summer. In winter it has prominent buds. Height: 45–60 cm (1½–2 ft) Spread: 50–60 cm (20–24 in)
- *Chamaecyparis lawsoniana* **'Little Spire':** hardy, slow-growing, evergreen conifer with an irregular but spire-like outline packed with dark blue-green foliage. Height: 1.5–2.4 m (5–8 ft) Spread: 30–60 cm (1–2 ft)
- *Chamaecyparis lawsoniana* **'Minima Aurea':** hardy, rounded, evergreen, dwarf conifer with bright yellow foliage. Height: 50–60 cm (20–24 in) Spread: 60–75 cm (2–2½ ft)
- *Juniperus communis* **'Golden Showers':** hardy, evergreen, slow-growing, upright conifer with a slightly feathery, column-like habit. In winter the foliage is yellowish-bronze, while in late spring and throughout summer it becomes bright golden-yellow. Height: 1.2–1.5 m (4–5 ft) Spread: 30–45 cm (1–1½ ft)
- *Juniperus communis* **'Hibernica' (Irish Juniper):** hardy, slow-growing, evergreen conifer, eventually upright and forming a large shrub. It has needle-like, greyish-blue foliage. Height: 1.8–2.1 m (6–7 ft) Spread: 40–50 cm (16–20 in)
- *Picea pungens* **'Iseli Fastigiate':** hardy, upright, slow-growing, evergreen, blue spruce densely packed with blue-green needles that in summer become bright blue. Initially it has a narrow, columnar nature, but with age broadens slightly. Height: 1–1.8 m (3½–6 ft) Spread: 45–60 cm (1½–2 ft)
- *Thuja occidentalis* **'Smaragd':** hardy, slow-growing, narrowly pyramidal, evergreen conifer with bright, rich green leaves that retain their attractive nature throughout winter. Height: 1.5–2.4 m (5–8 ft) Spread: 30–45 cm (1–1½ ft)
- *Thuja orientalis* **'Aurea Nana':** hardy, distinctive, evergreen, slow-growing conifer with a round to cone-shaped outline, packed with yellow-green foliage that turns gold in winter. Height: 60–75 cm (2–2½ ft) Spread: 50 cm (20 in)

Wall shrubs

*Why grow
shrubs
against walls?*

Apart from brightening a wall with leaves and flowers – often during winter and early spring when colour is least seen and is most welcome in gardens – against a wall is an ideal way to grow tender shrubs. Walls also enable more shrubs to be grown in small gardens. Many shrubs need a warm, wind-sheltered wall, while a few favour shade from strong sunlight that rapidly thaws frost-covered flowers. This includes *Jasminum nudiflorum* (Winter-flowering Jasmine).

WALL-SHRUB COMBINATIONS

Where space allows, plant the scrambling and bushy, hardy but often semi-evergreen, purple-blue and yellow-centred flowering shrub *Solanum crispum* 'Glasnevin' (Chilean Potato Tree) on one side of a doorway, and match it up with a yellow-flowered Honeysuckle – such as *Lonicera tragophylla* (Chinese Woodbine) – on the other side.

For an early-summer colour combination, try planting the large-leaved Ivy *Hedera colchica* 'Dentata Variegata', with its attractively variegated foliage, where it will be able to clamber over and through the half-hardy, evergreen wall shrub *Ceanothus cuneatus* var. *rigidus* (also known as *Ceanothus rigidus*), which produces clusters of small, violet flowers during late spring. This Ceanothus is an ideal shrub for planting in a restricted area against a sheltered wall.

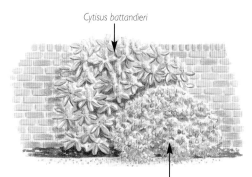

Cytisus battandieri

Evergreen Ceanothus

The gloriously blue flowers of Ceanothus *(Californian Lilac) are highlighted by the golden-yellow flowers of* Cytisus battandieri.

Abutilon megapotamicum

Half-hardy, slender-stemmed, evergreen or semi-evergreen wall shrub with bright green leaves and pendent, conspicuous, red and yellow flowers – with purple anthers – throughout summer and into early autumn.

Soil and position: light, well-drained soil and a warm position in the shelter of a wall and in full sun. It will grow in light shade, but the situation has to be extra warm.

Pruning: cut out winter-damaged and frost-damaged shoot tips in spring.

↕ 1.5–2.1 m (5–7 ft) ↔ 1.5–2.1 m (5–7 ft)

Ceanothus thyrsiflorus var. repens

Blue Blossom (USA)
Californian Lilac (UK)

Evergreen, mound-forming shrub that can be trained against a wall. During late spring and early summer it bears small, light blue flowers in 7.5 cm (3 in) long clusters.

Soil and position: light, neutral to slightly acid, well-drained, moisture-retentive soil and sheltered position.

Pruning: shorten lateral shoots to two or three buds from the previous season's growth after the flowers fade.

↕ 1.2–1.5 m (4–5 ft) ↔ 1.5–1.8 m (5–6 ft)

Cotoneaster horizontalis

Fish-bone Cotoneaster (UK)
Herringbone Cotoneaster (UK)
Rock Cotoneaster (USA)

Hardy, low-growing and spreading deciduous shrub with a horizontal and upright habit. Branches have a herringbone pattern, with glossy, dark green leaves that become red in autumn. Pink flowers appear in early summer, followed by red berries which last well into winter.

Soil and position: well-drained soil in full sun or partial shade.

Pruning: no regular pruning is needed.

↕ 60–90 cm (2–3 ft) ↔ 1.2–1.8 m (4–6 ft)

Cytisus battandieri

Moroccan Broom (UK)
Pineapple Broom (UK/USA)

Large, bushy, deciduous shrub, best grown against a wall in cold, temperate regions. During late spring and early summer it bears magnificent golden-yellow, pineapple-scented flowers.

Soil and position: well-drained soil in full sun and in the shelter of a wall. Avoid excessively rich soils.

Pruning: no regular pruning is needed, other than cutting out long and straggly shoots as soon as the flowers fade.

⬆ 3–4.5 m (10–15 ft)　↔ 3–3.6 m (10–12 ft)

Escallonia 'Donard Seedling'

Hardy, evergreen or semi-evergreen shrub with arching branches bearing glossy, dark-green leaves. During early and mid-summer it bears masses of apple-blossom-pink flowers. There are many other hybrid Escallonias – but most are not as hardy as this shrub.

Soil and position: well-drained soil in full sun and against a warm wall. It grows well in soils containing chalk.

Pruning: no regular pruning is needed, other than cutting out old, flowered stems as soon as the flowers fade.

⬆ 1.5–2.4 m (5–8 ft)　↔ 1.5–1.8 m (5–6 ft)

Fremontodendron californicum

Also known as *Fremontia californica*, this slightly tender deciduous or semi-evergreen shrub has three-lobed, dull green leaves covered with a soft, brown down. Cup-shaped, golden-yellow flowers, up to 5 cm (2 in) wide, are borne throughout summer and into early autumn.

Soil and position: well-drained, sandy soil, full sun and a warm, wind-sheltered wall.

Pruning: no regular pruning is needed, other than the removal of winter-damaged shoots in spring.

⬆ 1.8–3 m (6–10 ft)　↔ 1.8–3 m (6–10 ft)

Garrya elliptica

Silk Tassel Bush (UK/USA)

Quick-growing, evergreen shrub. During late winter – sometimes earlier in mild areas – and early spring it bears long, drooping, grey-green catkins. Male plants give the best display.

Soil and position: well-drained but moisture-retentive soil in full sun and sheltered from cold wind. It will grow in shade, but the display is diminished.

Pruning: no regular pruning is needed, other than shortening straggly shoots in late spring.

⬆ 2.4–3 m (8–10 ft)　↔ 1.8–3 m (6–10 ft)

Jasminum nudiflorum

Winter-flowering Jasmine (UK)

Deciduous, lax, wall shrub with pliable stems that bear bright yellow flowers from late autumn to late spring. The flowers are borne on bare stems.

Soil and position: well-drained soil and a position against a sheltered wall. However, it also grows well against cold-facing walls.

Pruning: as soon as flowers fade in spring, cut back flowered shoots to 5–7.5 cm (2–3 in) of their base. Also, cut out thin, weak and congested shoots.

⬆ 1.8–2.1 m (6–7 ft)　↔ 1.8–2.1 m (6–7 ft)

OTHERS TO CONSIDER

- *Abeliophyllum distichum*: slightly tender deciduous shrub with almond-scented, white, pink-tinged flowers borne on leafless stems during late winter and early spring.
- *Azara microphylla*: tender evergreen shrub that produces clusters of chrome-yellow flowers during late winter and early spring.
- *Ceanothus* 'Delight' (Californian Lilac): hardy evergreen shrub with small, bright blue flowers in late spring and early summer.
- *Lonicera fragrantissima*: slightly tender, partially evergreen shrub with fragrant creamy-white flowers from mid-winter to early spring.
- *Piptanthus nepalensis* (Evergreen Laburnum): also known as *Piptanthus laburnifolius*, it is nearly evergreen and produces large, bright yellow, laburnum-like flowers during late spring. In cold areas, it becomes deciduous. Although slightly tender, it is a quick-growing shrub and well worth planting where it will not be too constrained.

Berried shrubs and trees

Are these plants easy to grow?

Those shrubs and trees that produce colourful berries or fruits are just as easy to grow as those that are grown for their flowers or attractive leaves. Indeed, most need little or no pruning, and once planted create magnificent displays for a number of years. Most of them are self-contained, and do not require a related plant growing nearby to assist in the production of berries. Where companion plants are needed, this is indicated below.

BERRIED TREASURE

Many house walls, whether they are colour-washed, white or left just as bare bricks, have a bland appearance and could therefore do with some brightening up. Wall shrubs can create plenty of extra colour – in summer, many parade colourful flowers and attractive leaves, but in autumn and sometimes into winter the colour is often provided by eye-catching berries. In a garden, berried shrubs and trees play an important role, either in shrub and mixed borders or as specimen trees in a lawn.

Both red and yellow berries borne on these Pyracantha *(Firethorn) plants are highlighted by the white wall of the house.*

Pyracantha 'Orange Glow'

Pyracantha atalantioides 'Aurea'

Cotoneaster horizontalis (see page 40)

Callicarpa bodinieri var. giraldii

Beautyberry (UK/USA)

Also known as *Callicarpa giraldii*, this hardy, deciduous shrub has lance-shaped, narrow, pale green leaves that, in autumn, assume red and yellow tints. Lilac flowers appear in mid- and late summer, followed in autumn by masses of dark lilac or pale violet fruits.

Soil and position: well-drained but moisture-retentive soil in full sun.

Pruning: in late winter, cut back the previous year's shoots to young wood.

↕ 1.2–1.8 m (4–6 ft)   ↔ 1.5–1.8 m (5–6 ft)

Chaenomeles speciosa

Cydonia (UK)
Flowering Quince (UK/USA)
Japanese Quince (UK/USA)
Japonica (UK)

Hardy, deciduous, twiggy shrub with bowl-shaped, scarlet to blood-red flowers. Greenish-yellow fruits in autumn; in mild seasons they last well into winter.

Soil and position: well-drained but moisture-retentive soil in full sun.

Pruning: little pruning is needed when grown as a bush in a border.

↕ 1.5–1.8 m (5–6 ft)   ↔ 1.5–1.8 m (5–6 ft)

Clerodendrum trichotomum

Glory-bower (USA)

Slow-growing, bushy, deciduous shrub or small bushy tree with mid-green, oval leaves. Clusters of white, fragrant flowers appear from mid-summer to early autumn, followed by bright blue, later black, berries that persist into early winter.

Soil and position: fertile, well-drained soil in a wind-sheltered, sunny position.

Pruning: no regular pruning is needed, except to cut off frost-damaged shoot tips in spring.

↕ 3–4.5 m (10–15 ft)   ↔ 3–3.6 m (10–12 ft)

Cotoneaster lacteus

Hardy, evergreen shrub with shiny, deep green, oval, leathery leaves with hairy, grey undersides. Creamy-white flowers appear during early and mid-summer, followed by large clusters of red berries that persist well into winter.

Soil and position: well-drained but moisture-retentive soil in full sun or light shade.

Pruning: no regular pruning is needed.

⬆ 3–4.5 m (10–15 ft) ↔ 2.4–3.6 m (8–12 ft)

Gaultheria mucronata

Also known as *Pernettya mucronata*, this hardy, evergreen shrub has small, glossy, dark green leaves. White flowers appear in late spring or early summer, followed in autumn by fruits which range from white to pink, purple and red. They persist throughout winter. Both male and female plants must be present to produce berries.

Soil and position: lime-free, moisture-retentive soil, preferably in full sun. Also grows in light shade.

Pruning: no regular pruning is needed.

⬆ 60–90 cm (2–3 ft) ↔ 90 cm–1.5 m (3–5 ft)

Ilex aquifolium
Common Holly (UK)
English Holly (USA)

Hardy, evergreen large shrub or small tree with leathery, thick, glossy, dark green and almost spineless leaves. In winter it bears large crops of red fruits. It creates a dramatic feature in winter.

Soil and position: well-drained but moisture-retentive soil in full sun.

Pruning: no regular pruning is needed.

Warning: Do not eat the berries.

⬆ 3–4.5 m (10–15 ft) ↔ 1.8–3 m (6–10 ft)

Malus x zumi
'Golden Hornet'
Ornamental Crab Apple (UK)

Also known as *Malus* 'Golden Hornet', this hardy, deciduous, open and erect ornamental tree has pale green leaves. It reveals white flowers in late spring and early summer, followed by bright yellow fruits that often remain until mid-winter.

Soil and position: fertile, well-drained but moisture-retentive soil in full sun or partial shade.

Pruning: no regular pruning is needed.

⬆ 4.5–5.4 m (15–18 ft) ↔ 3–4.5 m (10–15 ft)

OTHERS TO CONSIDER

- *Cotoneaster conspicuus* **'Decorus'**: small, dense, evergreen shrub with oval, mid-green leaves. Flowers in early summer, followed in autumn by round, bright red berries which last through much of winter.
- *Cotoneaster frigidus* **'Cornubia'**: also known as *Cotoneaster* 'Cornubia', this hardy, semi-evergreen shrub has heavy clusters of red berries which last well into winter.
- *Cotoneaster microphyllus*: hardy, low, wide-spreading, evergreen shrub with scarlet berries that persist into winter, ideal for covering bare banks.
- *Cotoneaster salicifolius*: hardy, tall, evergreen shrub with willow-like, glossy-green, narrow leaves and bright red berries.
- *Hippophae rhamnoides*: hardy, bushy, large, deciduous shrub with stems and branches clothed with spines, and narrow, silvery leaves. If male and female plants are grown together, females bear bright orange berries in autumn and winter.
- *Ilex* x *altaclerensis* **'Golden King'**: hardy, evergreen large shrub or small tree with variegated leaves and large, red berries.
- *Malus* x *robusta* **'Red Sentinel'** (Ornamental Crab Apple): hardy, deciduous tree, also known as *Malus* 'Red Sentinel', with bright, deep red fruits that remain throughout winter.
- *Pyracantha atalantioides* (Firethorn): hardy, evergreen shrub with crimson berries that persist until early spring. The form 'Flava' has yellow berries.
- *Ruscus aculeatus* (Butcher's Broom): hardy, evergreen shrub with sealing-wax red berries that persist into early winter. Both male and female plants are essential for berries.
- *Symphoricarpos albus* **var.** *laevigatus* (Snowberry): hardy, deciduous, thicket-forming shrub with round, white berries until late winter.
- *Viburnum davidii*: small, hardy, evergreen shrub with bright turquoise-blue berries. Both male and female plants are essential for the production of berries.
- *Viburnum opulus* **'Xanthocarpum'**: hardy, deciduous shrub with translucent, rich yellow autumn fruits.

Bamboos and palms

Some bamboos are extremely invasive, and when established may trespass into neighbouring gardens; others are non-invasive. For each bamboo featured on these pages, an indication of its nature and vigour is given. If you are worried, the spread of the roots of a bamboo can be controlled by digging a metal barrier into the soil, to a depth of 50 cm (20 in) and protruding about 7.5 cm (3 in) above the surface. Never plant an invasive bamboo in a small area.

BAMBOOS FOR CONTAINERS

Some of the less invasive bamboos are ideal for growing in containers on a patio. In addition to *Fargesia murielae, Fargesia nitida, Phyllostachys nigra, Pleioblastus viridistriatus* and *Pseudosasa japonica*, which are all described in detail on these pages, two low-growing ones are:

• *Pleioblastus pygmaeus* (**Dwarf Fern-leaf Bamboo**): this bamboo has slender canes, a neat, dwarf habit and brilliant green leaves.

• *Pleioblastus variegatus* (**Dwarf White-striped Bamboo**): this bamboo has a dwarf habit and pale green canes. The upper surface of each individual leaf is dark green, striped with white and fading to paler green.

Fargesia murielae

Phyllostachys nigra

Pleioblastus viridistriatus

Bamboos, with their wide colour and height range, introduce an exciting feature into a garden, whatever its size.

Fargesia murieliae
Umbrella Bamboo (UK/USA)
Clump-forming and non-invasive.
Also known as *Arundinaria murieliae*, this hardy, elegant, clump-forming, graceful evergreen bamboo has arching, bright green canes that mature to dull yellow-green. The narrowly oblong, dark green leaves resemble those of *Fargesia nitida*.
Soil and position: fertile, moisture-retentive but well-drained soil in full sun or light shade.
Pruning: no pruning is needed.

⬆ 1.8–2.4 m (6–8 ft)

Fargesia nitida
Fountain Bamboo (UK/USA)
Queen of the Arundinarias (UK/USA)
Clump-forming and non-invasive.
Also known as *Arundinaria nitida* and *Sinoarundinaria nitida*, this fast-growing, hardy evergreen has purple stems covered with a waxy bloom. The narrow, bright green, lance-shaped leaves rustle attractively in the wind.
Soil and position: fertile, moisture-retentive but well-drained soil in full sun or light shade.
Pruning: no pruning is needed.

⬆ 3.6–4.5 m (12–15 ft)

Phyllostachys nigra
Black-stemmed Bamboo (UK/USA)
Black Bamboo (UK/USA)
Moderately invasive but easily checked.
Hardy, graceful, evergreen, clump-forming bamboo with canes first green then jet black within 2–3 years. The dark green leaves are about 13 cm (5 in) long and 12 mm (½ in) wide.
Soil and position: fertile, moisture-retentive but well-drained soil in full sun. The stems achieve their best colours when in dry soil.
Pruning: no pruning is needed.

⬆ 2.4–3 m (8–10 ft)

Pleioblastus viridistriatus

Golden-haired Bamboo (UK/USA)

Moderately invasive but can be checked.

Also known as *Pleioblastus auricomus*, this is a superb hardy, dwarf bamboo with slender, purple-green stems and 20 cm (8 in) long and 42 mm (1¾ in) wide, brilliant golden-yellow leaves with pea-green stripes.

Soil and position: plant in fertile, moisture-retentive but well-drained soil in good light; this is important to encourage the best coloured leaves.

Pruning: no pruning is needed.

↕ 90 cm–1.2 m (3–4 ft)

Pseudosasa japonica

Arrow Bamboo (UK/USA)
Metake (UK/USA)

Moderately invasive but can be checked.

Also known as *Arundinaria japonica*, this hardy, evergreen bamboo has sharply pointed, oblong to lance-shaped, dark glossy-green leaves. It forms a large thicket and is ideal for screening as well as to form a hedge.

Soil and position: fertile, moisture-retentive but well-drained soil in full sun or light shade.

Pruning: no pruning is needed.

↕ 2.4–3.5 m (8–15 ft)

Sasa veitchii

Kuma Bamboo Grass (USA)

Spreading and invasive.

Also known as *Arundinaria veitchii*, this hardy, invasive and low-growing bamboo has slender, purple-green canes. The glossy, smooth-surfaced leaves, to 25 cm (10 in) long and about 6 cm (2½ in) wide, are deep rich-green and with withered edges and tips during winter; they have an attractive papery nature.

Soil and position: fertile, moisture-retentive but well-drained soil in dappled light.

Pruning: no pruning is needed.

↕ 90 cm–1.5 m (3–5 ft)

OTHER BAMBOOS

- *Chimonobambusa quadrangularis* (**Square-stemmed Bamboo**): also known as *Arundinaria quadrangularis* and *Bambusa quadrangularis*, this robust, sometimes rampant, hardy bamboo has square, dark-green stems, occasionally splashed purple. Deep olive-green leaves up to 23 cm (9 in) long. It has an invasive nature.
- *Phyllostachys aurea* (**Fishpole Bamboo**): hardy, graceful bamboo with bright green canes maturing to dull yellow when in full sun. The leaves are light pea-green; young shoots are edible in spring. It is moderately invasive, but easily checked.
- *Phyllostachys bambusoides* 'Castilloni' (**Golden Brilliant Bamboos**): also known as *Phyllostachys castillonis*, this hardy, graceful, very attractive bamboo has rich golden-yellow stems with vivid green grooves. The bright green leaves are 7.5–15 cm (3–6 in) long and about 12 mm (½ in) wide. It is moderately invasive, but can be easily checked.
- *Pseudosasa amabilis* (**Tonkin Bamboo**): also known as *Arundinaria amabilis*, this beautiful, moderately cold-resistant bamboo has tough, mid-green, thick-walled but pliable canes that arch at their ends. The bright green leaves vary in length from 10 to 30 cm (4–12 in) and up to 36 mm (1½ in) wide. It is moderately invasive, but can be easily checked.
- *Sasaella ramosa* (**Dwarf Bamboo**): also known as *Arundinaria ramosa*, this hardy, exceedingly rampant and vigorous ground-covering bamboo has bright green canes that mature to deep olive. The mid-green leaves, dull greyish-green beneath, are about 15 cm (6 in) long and 18 mm (¾ in) wide. It is ideal for covering banks and large areas. It is spreading and invasive.

PALMS

In general, palms are not frost-hardy plants, but there is one that grows well in temperate climates – Trachycarpus fortunei *(Chinese Windmill Palm).*

Trachycarpus fortunei (**Chinese Windmill Palm, Chusan Palm, Windmill Palm**): Slow-growing palm with large fans, often 90 cm (3 ft) wide and formed of narrow, folded segments on stalks up to 90 cm (3 ft) long. Additionally, the trunk is clothed in black, coarse, hairy fibre that creates another attractive quality.

Soil and position: well-drained but moisture-retentive soil in full sun and light shade. No pruning is needed.

Height: 3–3.6 m (10–12 ft) **Spread:** 1.8–3 m (6–10 ft)

Hedges for boundaries

Are all hedges formal?

There are many superb formal hedging shrubs and trees, ranging from the evergreen *Taxus baccata* (Yew) to the deciduous *Fagus sylvatica* (Beech). Others have an informal outline that makes them ideal for relaxed gardens, perhaps with a cottage-garden feel. The evergreen *Berberis* x *stenophylla* provides an informal outline as a boundary hedge, while *Lonicera nitida* 'Baggesen's Gold' can either be left to create informality or be clipped into a formal shape.

OTHER BOUNDARY HEDGES

The range of plants that are suitable for growing as formal and informal boundary hedges is wide, and includes:

- *Griselinia littoralis*: dense, evergreen shrub, ideal for coastal areas.
- *Taxus baccata* (English Yew): conifer, formal and evergreen.
- *Thuja plicata*: conifer, formal and evergreen.

HEIGHTS AND WIDTHS

The heights and widths given for these hedges are those when clipped.

By using the all-green and yellow-leaved Privet, you can create a two-tone hedge.

Tall, evergreen hedges create privacy and seclusion, but need regular clipping.

Cupressus macrocarpa 'Golden Cone'
Monterey Cypress (UK/USA)

Hardy, evergreen, robust, fast-growing, dense conifer with bright green foliage. It is ideal for creating a boundary in an exposed area. Young plants, however, can be difficult to establish.

Soil and position: well-drained but moisture-retentive soil in full sun. Space plants 45–60 cm (1½–2 ft) apart.

Pruning: Clip the hedge several times during summer.

↕ 1.8–3m (6–10 ft) ↔ 1–1.2m (3½–4 ft)

Ligustrum ovalifolium
Californian Privet (USA)
Common Privet (UK)

Hardy, bushy, evergreen shrub, but can become partially evergreen in exposed and cold areas. it has oval, glossy, mid-green leaves that create a colour-neutral background. *Ligustrum ovalifolium* 'Aureum' has yellow leaves.

Soil and position: ordinary well-drained but moisture-retentive soil in full sun or partial shade. Space plants of the species 30–45 cm (12–18 in) apart; space the yellow-leaved form 30–38 cm (12–15 in) apart.

Pruning: clip hedges several times during summer.

↕ 1.2–1.8 m (4–6 ft) ↔ 60–75 cm (2–2½ ft)

Lonicera nitida 'Baggesen's Gold'
Yellow-leaved Chinese Honeysuckle (UK)

Hardy, bushy, evergreen shrub with small, golden-yellow leaves which become yellowish-green in late summer or autumn. It is slightly less vigorous than the all-green form.

Soil and position: well-drained but moisture-retentive soil in full sun. Plant 25 cm (10 in) apart.

Pruning: it is best grown as an informal hedge, rather than regular clipping.

↕ 90 cm–1.2 m (3–4 ft) ↔ 45–60 cm (1½–2 ft)

Internal hedges

The range of small, flowering hedges for planting within a garden is wide, from *Lavandula angustifolia* 'Hidcote' (Lavender) to *Potentilla fruticosa* (Shrubby Cinquefoil). Additionally, some shrubs, such as the diminutive evergreen *Santolina chamaecyparissus*, have both attractive foliage and flowers. *Rosmarinus* (Rosemary), which has a cottage-garden nature, also forms a magnificent hedge and steeps a garden in rich, aromatic fragrance as well as flowers.

Are there many small flowering hedges?

LAVENDER HEDGE

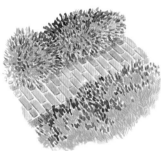

With its informal and cottage-garden nature, aromatic Lavender is ideal for planting alongside a rustic path.

Lavandula angustifolia 'Hidcote'
Lavender (UK/USA)

Also known as *Lavandula nana* var. *atropurpurea*, this hardy, evergreen shrub forms a low-growing, relatively short-lived hedge that is ideal for planting alongside an informal path. The narrow, silvery-grey leaves are surmounted by deep purple-blue flowers.

Soil and position: well-drained but moisture-retentive soil, a sheltered position and full sun. Space plants 23–30 cm (9–12 in) apart.

Pruning: clip established hedges during early to mid-spring.

⬆ 45–60 cm (18–24 in) ↔ 45–60 cm (18–24 in)

Potentilla fruticosa
Shrubby Cinquefoil (UK/USA)

Hardy, deciduous, bushy but compact shrub with masses of buttercup-yellow flowers from early to late summer – and sometimes later. There are several hybrids, some with red flowers.

Soil and position: light, well-drained but moisture-retentive soil in full sun. Space plants 30–38 cm (12–15 in) apart.

Pruning: no regular clipping is needed, other than removing dead flowerheads.

⬆ 90 cm–1.2 m (3–4 ft) ↔ 45–60 cm (1½–2 ft)

Buxus sempervirens 'Suffruticosa'
Dwarf Edging Box (UK/USA)

Hardy, dwarf, hedging shrub, ideal for a neat, clipped, miniature edging around borders. Small, dark green and glossy leaves cluster around stems.

Soil and position: well-drained but moisture-retentive soil in full sun. Space plants 15–20 cm (6–8 in) apart.

Pruning: clip the hedge several times during summer.

⬆ 23–30 cm (9–12 in) ↔ 20–25 cm (8–10 in)

OTHER INTERNAL HEDGES

- *Berberis thunbergii* 'Atropurpurea Nana': compact and deciduous, with reddish-purple leaves.
- *Fuchsia magellanica*: a slightly tender shrub that bears crimson and purple flowers.
- *Rosa* 'White Pet': also known as *Rosa* 'Little White Pet', this Polyantha Rose creates a hedge about 60 cm (2 ft) high, and produces small, white, pompon-like flowers.

Occasionally, a tall internal hedge may be needed to protect tender plants.

Shrubs and trees in borders

Is detailed planning essential?

Once planted, a new shrub border will be with you for many years. Even though you may be keen to get the border established, therefore, careful planning is essential to ensure that problems do not arise during later years. In the plant directory on pages 18–47, the expected size of each shrub and tree after 15–20 years is indicated. Do not attempt to cram in masses of shrubs, although it is possible to plant a few as temporary fillers.

PLANTING A SHRUB BORDER

3 *Stand the shrubs, still in their containers, in position. Starting from the back of the border, plant each shrub (see pages 10–11 for details). Make sure that the most attractive side of each plant is facing towards the front of the border. When all the planting is complete, thoroughly but gently water the soil and add a mulch.*

1 *When planning a new shrub border, first make a scale drawing of the bed. Then write the names of the shrubs you want on separate pieces of paper, and arrange these on the drawing.*

2 *Transfer the plan to a prepared border and use lines of sharp sand to mark the planting areas. It is possible to use a sharp stick, and this works well if the soil remains damp.*

PRICKLY CUSTOMERS!

The range of qualities exhibited by shrubs and trees is wide, and while many are famed for their flowers and leaves others are noted for their prickles and spines.
- *Genista hispanica* (Spanish Gorse): hardy, deciduous, densely spined and branched shrub.
- *Gleditsia triacanthos* (Honey Locust): hardy, deciduous tree armed with spines.
- *Robinia pseudoacacia* (False Acacia): hardy, deciduous tree with short spines at the leaf-joints.
- *Ulex europaeus* 'Flore Pleno' (Double-flowered Gorse): hardy, evergreen, densely spined shrub.

A RANGE OF SHRUBS AND TREES

FLOWERING SHRUBS AND TREES
For flower colour throught the year, see pages 18–27.
- Wide range of flowering shrubs, from plants 15 cm (6 in) high to ones 2.4 m (8 ft) or more.
- Colour, shape and size variation – additionally, some shrubs have fragrant flowers and are especially welcome during the winter months.

FOLIAGE SHRUBS AND TREES
These introduce colour over a long period.
- For leaf colour from spring to autumn, plant deciduous shrubs and trees. Some are especially attractive in spring, and others in autumn (see pages 28–29).
- For leaf colour throughout the year, plant evergreen shrubs and trees (see pages 32–35).

COLOURED BARK AND STEMS
These create attractive features throughout the year (see pages 30–31).
- Some trees with coloured bark, such as *Betula pendula* (Silver Birch), are superb when planted in small groups.
- Trees with dominantly coloured trunks, such as *Acer griseum* (Paperbark Maple), are ideal when featured individually on lawns.

DECIDUOUS SHRUBS AND TREES
These lose their leaves in autumn, but nevertheless create dramatic displays.
- Single-coloured leaves – from yellow to soft purple and silver.
- Variegated leaves are varied, from combinations of yellow and white to red and purple.
- When unfurling in spring, the colours of some leaves are intensified.

A RANGE OF SHRUBS AND TREES (CONTINUED)

EVERGREEN SHRUBS AND TREES
Consider evergreen plants when colour throughout the year is desired (see pages 32–35).
- Some plants have single-coloured leaves and because of this often create a thick screen of dominant foliage.
- Variegated leaves have many colour combinations, but mainly within the green, white, cream and yellow range.

DECIDUOUS CONIFERS
There are fewer deciduous conifers than evergreen types (see pages 36–37).
- Some deciduous conifers, such as *Larix decidua* (European Larch), are ideal for planting in a large lawn and have especially attractive leaves in spring.
- Several deciduous conifers, such as *Metasequoia glyptostroboides* (Dawn Redwood), have colourful autumn leaves.

EVERGREEN CONIFERS
The range is wide, from slow-growing and dwarf types (see pages 38–39) to large and dominant ones (see pages 36–37).
- Select large conifers with care, as eventually they may form dominant, permanent parts of a garden's landscape.
- Dwarf conifers remain small, but slow-growing types eventually will need to be dug up and moved.

BAMBOOS
These evergreen plants have a distinctive nature, with attractive canes and leaves (see pages 44–45).
- Bamboos are usually planted in shrub borders, although they can be used to form screens and ground cover. Also, some can be planted in containers.
- Some bamboos have exceptionally attractive canes, in a wide range of colours and shapes.

AUTUMN-COLOURED SHRUBS AND TREES
These deciduous plants create dramatic features (see pages 28–29).
- There are many autumn-coloured shrubs, such as *Fothergilla major*, that are ideal for small gardens.
- Some trees, such as *Liquidambar styraciflua* (Sweet Gum), are ideal for planting as a focal point in a large lawn.

BERRIED SHRUBS AND TREES
Several evergreen and deciduous shrubs and trees produce berries (see pages 42–43).
- Berries attract birds, but shrubs often escape the attention of birds better than trees do.
- Ensure that berried trees are not positioned where branches overhang paths – fallen berries when trodden upon create a slippery surface.

SCENTED SHRUBS AND TREES

It is possible to have more than 100 different fragrances in a garden, created mainly from flowers and leaves and often by shrubs and trees. Sweetness is the most common scent, but unusual ones range from almond to orange blossom.
- **Almond:** *Prunus padus* 'Watereri' (Bird Cherry). Long, drooping tassels of white, almond-scented flowers in late spring and often into early summer.
- **Cowslip:** *Corylopsis pauciflora*. Pale primrose-yellow, bell-shaped flowers in drooping clusters during spring.
- **Honey:** *Ulex europaeus* 'Flore Pleno' (Double-flowered Gorse). Honey-scented, golden-yellow flowers, mainly in late spring and early summer – and often intermittently throughout summer and into winter.
- **Lemon:** *Magnolia sieboldii*. Cup-shaped, white flowers with claret-red stamens, from early to late summer.
- **Lily-of-the-valley:** *Skimmia japonica* 'Fragrans'. Dense clusters of small, star-like, white flowers during late spring.
- **Orange-blossom:** *Philadelphus* (Mock Orange). White, cup-shaped flowers during early and mid-summer.

POSITIONING FRAGRANT SHRUBS AND TREES

Gardens steeped in rich and unusual fragrances are memorable. In all gardens – whatever their size or shape – there are places in which scented shrubs and trees can be grown. Here are a few places to consider.

Arches: most arches are packed with climbers but *Laburnum* x *watereri*, which is usually grown as a tree, can be trained to form an arch or tunnel. In early summer it develops sweetly scented, pendulous clusters of golden-yellow flowers. Creating a floriferous arch takes several years.

Borders: shrub and mixed borders invariably benefit from the inclusion of a few fragrant shrubs. The range is wide, but make sure a few winter-flowering types are present. These include *Hamamelis mollis* (Chinese Witch Hazel), with sweet, golden-yellow flowers, and *Mahonia* x *media* 'Charity', lemon-yellow and sweet.

Walls: several wall shrubs are richly scented, including *Cytisus battandieri* (Moroccan Broom) and *Chimonanthus praecox* (Winter Sweet).

Mixed borders

*What are
mixed
borders?*

Mixed borders comprise a medley of plants, with shrubs and small trees creating the main framework and the spaces between them filled with herbaceous perennials, bulbs, tuberous plants such as Dahlias, annuals and biennials. Because mixed borders are formed of many different types of plants, they are well able to create colour throughout the year. Even during winter, when frost covers stems and leaves, the border is full of eye appeal.

WHAT IS THE VALUE OF A MIXED BORDER?

In small gardens, mixed borders are especially useful because they create homes for a wide range of plants that otherwise – perhaps for space reasons – could not be grown. They have a natural and plant-packed appearance throughout the year, rather than seasonal displays in summer-flowering beds packed with half-hardy annuals, or herbaceous borders with plants that mainly flower from spring to late autumn. Mixed borders frequently evoke the charm of a cottage garden.

SHOULD THE BORDER FACE THE SUN?

Most gardeners have no choice about the orientation of a border, but whether it faces the sun or otherwise there are advantages and disadvantages. Borders facing the sun are invariably earlier-flowering and can contain tender plants. Additionally, leaves will not be damaged so readily by cold winds. Borders facing cold aspects have colder soil during winter, and therefore are later in their display. However, because there is little sun, frost-covered flowers are not at such risk from the danger of sudden thawing.

A MIXED BORDER IN SUMMER

This border is packed with summer colour. It is illustrated again on the opposite page during spring, autumn and winter, when other plants are in flower.

Lonicera japonica

Berberis thunbergii 'Atropurpurea Nana'

Phormium

Camellia

Rhododendron

Rudbeckia

Skimmia japonica

Alchemilla mollis

Erica carnea

Pinus mugo Pumilio Group

Hosta

Lavandula

Vinca minor

THROUGH THE SEASONS

The main illustration on these pages shows a mixed border during summer. The illustrations below depict the same border at different times of the year.

Spring

↙ *Spring is full of vitality and new growth, with many early-flowering plants revealing colour.*

Autumn

↙ *Autumn is often considered to be an afterthought, but in this border variegated shrubs continue the colour.*

Winter

↙ *Winter reveals winter-flowering Pansies, berried shrubs and those plants with a display of variegated leaves.*

HOW LONG WILL A MIXED BORDER LAST?

After initial planting, a mixed border will last 3–4 years before the herbaceous plants need to be lifted, divided and replanted. The shrubs and trees (if pruned and looked after) will remain attractive and healthy for ten or more years.

IS IT MORE EXPENSIVE TO PLANT A MIXED BORDER THAN ONE COMPLETELY FORMED OF SHRUBS?

Individually, shrubs and small trees are more expensive to buy than herbaceous plants. Also, bulbs such as Daffodils and Tulips can be bought specially for planting and naturalizing in mixed borders. However, bulbs that have finished flowering indoors or been in containers on a patio can be reused in a mixed border, as can spare summer-flowering bedding plants left over after planting up container displays.

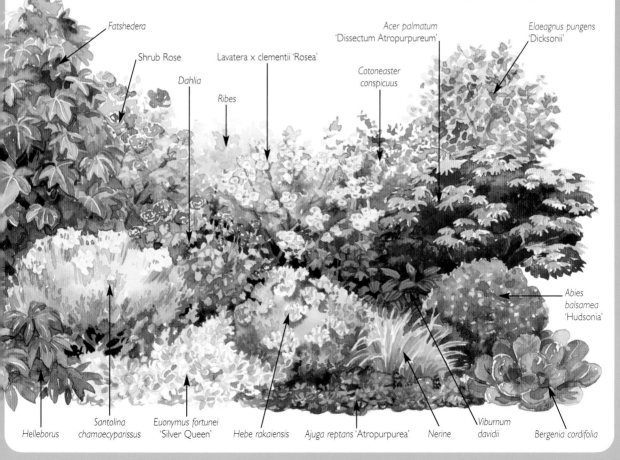

Fatshedera

Shrub Rose

Dahlia

Lavatera × clementii 'Rosea'

Ribes

Cotoneaster conspicuus

Acer palmatum 'Dissectum Atropurpureum'

Elaeagnus pungens 'Dicksonii'

Abies balsamea 'Hudsonia'

Helleborus

Santolina chamaecyparissus

Euonymus fortunei 'Silver Queen'

Hebe rakaiensis

Ajuga reptans 'Atropurpurea'

Nerine

Viburnum davidii

Bergenia cordifolia

Growing shrubs and trees in containers

Which containers are best?

When growing shrubs and trees in containers, it is essential to ensure that they cannot be blown over by strong wind. For this reason, containers need to be matched in size to the proportions of the shrub or tree – tubs enable large shrubs and trees to be grown. Remember that evergreen shrubs will be more at risk than deciduous types of being blown over during blustery winter weather. Soil-based compost gives greater stability than peat-based types.

This conifer has a dignified character – put small, summer-flowering plants around it.

CREATING A MIXED DISPLAY

Fatsia japonica

Acer palmatum 'Dissectum atropurpureum'

Choisya ternata 'Sundance'

Yucca filamentosa 'Variegata'

Kurume Azalea

Hebe × franciscana 'Variegata'

This medley of shrubs in containers brings welcome colour to an otherwise dull patio.

WHAT ARE THE ADVANTAGES OF SHRUBS AND SMALL TREES IN CONTAINERS?

- Plants can be positioned where they will create a good display – perhaps close to the house and easily seen from a window.
- More plant space is created in small gardens and on patios.
- There is the opportunity of 'mixing and matching' plants in a small area – trying different combinations creates added eye appeal.
- You can get 'double-value' gardening – plants which outgrow a container can be planted into a border.
- Large shrubs and trees will create focal points on patios and are ideal for backing groups of smaller container-grown plants.
- Tubs can be used to direct foot traffic on patios, perhaps away from open casement windows.

WATERING

Shrubs and trees when established and growing in borders usually thrive without any additional water being given to them, except in very dry seasons, but those in tubs and large pots need regular attention.

- During the summer, at least once a day check that the compost is evenly moist – neither dry nor waterlogged.
- In the autumn, reduce the amount and frequency of watering, especially for deciduous shrubs and trees.
- Shrubs and trees, when they are in flower, will soon suffer if the compost is dry.

WHAT ARE THE DISADVANTAGES OF SHRUBS AND SMALL TREES IN CONTAINERS?

- Shrubs and trees in tubs and pots need regular watering throughout summer.
- Tender evergreen shrubs need protection in winter, sometimes by enveloping the foliage in straw. Alternatively, they can be moved into a greenhouse or conservatory.
- In winter, wet compost soon freezes and may damage the roots of plants – prevent the compost become too wet by placing plastic sheeting over it (but be sure to remove it in late winter).
- Time and effort will be required to remove and plant a shrub or tree when it grows too big for a tub or large pot.
- There is the risk of the container being blown over by gusty wind in winter.

SHRUBS FOR CONTAINERS

Acer palmatum 'Dissectum Atropurpureum'	Hardy, slow-growing, deciduous tree with finely dissected, bronze-red leaves on a plant with a low, rounded habit.
Aucuba japonica 'Variegata' Gold Dust Tree/Spotted Laurel	Hardy, evergreen shrub with shiny, dark green leaves spotted and splashed in yellow. It is especially attractive in winter.
Buxus sempervirens 'Suffruticosa' Dwarf Edging Box	Hardy, evergreen shrub with small, glossy, dark green leaves that tightly cluster around stems.
Camellia x williamsii	Evergreen shrub, mainly flowering in late winter and spring. Many varieties, in colours from white and pale pink to rose-purple.
Choisya ternata 'Sundance' Yellow-leaved Mexican Orange Blossom	Slightly tender evergreen shrub with glossy, golden-yellow leaves. From late spring to early summer it bears faintly orange-blossom scented white flowers.
Fatsia japonica False Castor Oil Plant/ Japanese Fatsia	Slightly tender, evergreen shrub with large, glossy, hand-like leaves with coarsely toothed edges. In autumn and into winter it bears white flowers.
Hebe x andersonii 'Variegata' Shrubby Veronica	Slightly tender evergreen shrub with cream and green leaves. Lavender flowers appear from mid-summer to autumn.
Hebe x franciscana 'Variegata' Shrubby Veronica	Slightly tender evergreen shrub with glossy-green leaves edged in cream. Additionally, it bears mauve-blue flowers.
Hypericum olympicum	Hardy, low-growing evergreen shrub with golden-yellow flowers during mid-summer. It has a slightly domed, spreading nature.
Laurus nobilis Bay	Hardy, evergreen tree, often grown as a half-standard in a tub. The glossy, aromatic, mid-green leaves are added to food.
Lavandula angustifolia 'Hidcote' Lavender	Hardy, evergreen shrub with narrow, silvery-grey leaves and deep purple-blue flowers from mid- to late summer.
Phormium tenax New Zealand Flax New Zealand Hemp	Half-hardy evergreen shrub with strap-like, leathery, mid- to deep green leaves. There are many forms, some with coloured or variegated leaves.
Rosmarinus officinalis Rosemary	Hardy, evergreen shrub with aromatic leaves and mauve flowers during spring - and intermittently throughout summer and sometimes into autumn.
Yucca filamentosa 'Variegata' Variegated Adam's Needle	Slightly tender evergreen shrub with rosettes of deep green leaves edged in whitish-yellow.

CONIFERS

Conifers growing in tubs or large pots need regular attention to ensure that the compost does not become either dry in summer or excessively wet in winter. Dry compost soon causes the foliage to become crisp and dry, and if this continues the plant loses its attractiveness. Conversely, compost that is waterlogged in winter causes the roots to decay, which may not be apparent until spring when the plant attempts to make new growth.

Chamaecyparis lawsoniana 'Ellwoodii'
Slow-growing, evergreen conifer with short, feather-like sprays of grey-green leaves that, in winter, assume shades of steel-blue.

Chamaecyparis lawsoniana 'Minima Aurea'
Dwarf, slow-growing, hardy, evergreen conifer with a rounded outline and sprays of soft, bright yellow leaves.

Chamaecyparis pisifera 'Filifera Aurea'
Slow-growing, evergreen conifer with spreading branches packed with thread-like, golden foliage.

Juniperus communis 'Compressa'
Slow-growing, hardy, evergreen conifer with a columnar nature and narrow, prickly, silver-backed leaves.

Juniperus communis 'Depressa Aurea'
Slow-growing evergreen conifer with a spreading nature and packed with bright yellow foliage when young.

Juniperus scopulorum 'Skyrocket'
Also known as *Juniperus virginiana* 'Skyrocket', this hardy, evergreen, slow-growing conifer has a narrow habit and blue-grey leaves.

Taxus baccata 'Standishii'
Slow-growing, hardy, evergreen conifer with a densely columnar habit and packed with golden-yellow leaves.

Thuja orientalis 'Aurea Nana'
Slow-growing, hardy, evergreen conifer with a neat, rounded habit and beautiful light yellow-green foliage that appears especially attractive when the tree is positioned in full sun.

Growing shrubs against walls

Can all shrubs be grown against a wall?

Many shrubs appreciate shelter from cold winds and the warmth generated by a sunny position near to a wall, without being planted and trained directly against one. Other shrubs, such as *Cotoneaster horizontalis* (Herringbone Cotoneaster), have a natural tendency to lean against a wall. Others may need a firm supporting framework or a system of wires to prevent them being either blown away from a wall or deformed under the weight of snow.

ESTABLISHING A WALL SHRUB

In order to encourage the rapid establishment of newly planted wall shrubs:
- do not plant them too close to a wall (the soil will be continually dry);
- mix in plenty of well-decomposed garden compost to the soil before planting;
- apply a mulch of well-decomposed garden compost;
- water them regularly.

Above: Climbers, as well as many shrubs, thrive in the warmth and shelter provided by a wall.
Left: Pyracanthas are hardy shrubs, with flowers during summer and berries that sometimes last right through the winter.

CAN I GROW APPLES AND PEARS AGAINST A WALL?

This is ideal in a small garden, where you will have the benefit of flowers in spring and fruit later. Plant either an espalier, or several cordons.
- A mature espalier apple will yield 9–13.6 kg (20–30 lb) of fruit each year, and an espalier pear 6.8–11.3 kg (15–25 lb).
- Cordon apples, planted 75 cm (2½ ft) apart, will each produce 2.2–3.1 kg (5–7 lb) of fruit.
- Cordon pears, also planted 75 cm (2½ ft) apart, yield 1.8–2.7 kg (4–6 lb) of fruit.

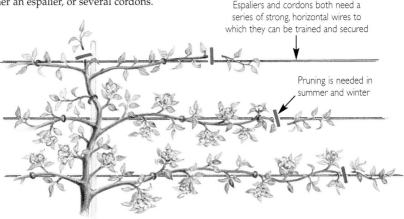

Espaliers and cordons both need a series of strong, horizontal wires to which they can be trained and secured

Pruning is needed in summer and winter

Growing Roses against walls

Roses are deciduous shrubs – both climbing and rambling types can be grown against walls.

Climbers have larger flowers than ramblers and more permanent growth. Also, they have the ability to repeat flowering after their first flush of flowers.

Ramblers differ from climbers in having long, flexible stems which develop mainly from the plant's base.

Four Roses for cold walls

• **'Albéric Barbier' (rambler):** yellow buds opening to fully double, creamy-white flowers in small clusters.

• **'Félicité Perpétue' (rambler):** large clusters of small, creamy-white flowers. The buds are tinted pink.

• **'Madame Grégoire Staechelin' (climber):** long, shapely buds, opening to semi-double, glowing-pink flowers with the fragrance of sweet peas.

• **'Zéphirine Drouhin' (climber):** fragrant, deep rose-pink flowers over a long period. It is one of the most reliable-flowering climbers.

ROSES FOR WALLS AND POOR SOIL

Usually it is possible to improve soil before climbing or rambling Roses are planted, as well as feeding and mulching afterwards. Should conditions be difficult and with little opportunity of improvement, however, try the following wall brighteners. Incidentally, climbing Roses succeed better than ramblers in impoverished soils.

• 'Cécile Brunner, Climbing': climber, with Hybrid Tea-type, blush-pink flowers. It is sweetly scented.

• 'Constance Spry': a New English Rose, often grown as a shrub but also successful as a climber. It develops large, myrrh-scented, soft pink flowers.

• 'Leverkusen': climber, with rosette-shaped, lemon-yellow flowers that emit the fragrance of lemons.

• 'Madame Alfred Carrière': climber, with large, sweetly scented, cup-shaped, white flowers tinted with flesh-pink. It is usually free from the risk of diseases.

• 'Maigold': climber, with large, semi-double, fragrant, bronze-yellow flowers with golden stamens. It is very hardy and well suited for poor conditions.

• 'Noisette Carnée' (also known as 'Blush Noisette'): climber, with clusters of small, cupped, semi-double, lilac-pink flowers with a clove-like fragrance.

Further wall shrubs to consider

In addition to the wall shrubs illustrated and described on pages 40–41, there are several others to consider; some of these especially require a warm wall.

• *Actinidia kolomikta* (**Kolomikta Vine**): a hardy, deciduous, climbing shrub grown for its magnificent leaves. They are heart-shaped and dark green, with varying amounts of pink or white towards the tip. Incidentally, cats are often attracted by it. Therefore, protect young plants.

• *Berberidopsis corallina* (**Coral Plant**): slightly tender, evergreen shrub, ideal for planting against a warm but shaded wall. It bears heart-shaped to oval, thick and leathery, spine-edged leaves. Deep crimson flowers appear in late summer.

• *Caesalpinia gilliesii* (**Bird of Paradise Shrub**): slightly tender deciduous shrub with rich yellow flowers and scarlet stamens during mid- and late summer. The leaves are formed of dainty leaflets.

• *Genista* '**Porlock**': also known as *Cytisus* 'Porlock', this slightly tender, semi-evergreen shrub needs the protection of a warm, sheltered wall. During spring it displays sweetly scented yellow flowers.

• *Magnolia grandiflora* (**Bull Bay/ Southern Magnolia**): slightly tender evergreen tree, best grown in the warmth and shelter of a wall. The leaves are large, oval and leathery, with creamy-white, bowl-shaped, fragrant flowers from mid-summer to early autumn. The form 'Exmouth' has large, richly fragrant flowers; they appear at an early stage in the plant's life.

• *Trachelospermum jasminoides* (**Confederate Jasmine/Star Jasmine**): slow-growing, evergreen climbing shrub best grown against a warm, wind-sheltered wall. The leaves are dark green and leathery, while the fragrant, white flowers appear during mid- and late summer.

Climbing and rambling Roses can be used to clothe walls with flowers, and they are available in a wide range of colours. Some also have captivating fragrances.

Specimen trees in lawns

Of what value are trees in lawns?

A specimen tree – whether flowering, bearing handsome foliage or with eye-catching bark – on a lawn creates an impression of well-being in a garden. It is rather like adding a distinctive decoration to a birthday cake. For a really memorable tree, you could plant one to commemorate a wedding or birth. If white lilac was used in a wedding bouquet, choose a standard white lilac. Such trees enrich gardens as well as recalling happy memories.

SINGLE OR IN GROUPS

Some trees – such as those with a uniform and formal outline – look best when on their own, while informal types are often better when in a small group.
- Single displays: choose distinctive trees, whether upright or weeping like *Picea breweriana* (Brewer's Spruce).
- In groups: small groups of trees – go for threes, rather than two or four – look magnificent and are ideal in an informal or irregularly shaped lawn. Three *Betula pendula* (Silver Birch) trees are superb when the bark is caught by low light.

WHAT MAKES A GOOD TREE FOR A LAWN?

Lawns, whether formal or informal, are enhanced by a tree planted about two-thirds of the way along its length. Select the tree carefully, considering all the following factors.

Size
Ensure that the tree does not dominate the lawn, in either height or width. Trees with clinical outlines will appear smaller than those with spreading branches.

Shape
Some trees have a casual outline, while others are clinical and symmetrical. Select a tree to suit the nature of the garden – formal or informal.

Trunk
There are two reasons for having a clear trunk: to enable the lawn to be easily cut close to the trunk, and to enable the garden beyond the tree to be seen.

Long-term interest
Select a tree that creates interest for as long a period as possible throughout the year. See below for a range of attractive qualities, from bark to leaves.

TREES FOR LAWNS

Acer davidii (**Snakebark Maple**) ~ deciduous tree with magnificent grey bark striped white.

Acer griseum (**Paperbark Maple**) ~ hardy, deciduous tree with buff-coloured bark and autumn-coloured leaves (illustrated on page 30).

Acer negundo '**Elegans**' (**Variegated Box Elder**) ~ also known as *Acer negundo* 'Elegantissimum', this hardy, deciduous, wide-spreading tree has leaves attractively variegated mid-green and bright yellow.

Acer platanoides '**Drummondii**' (**Variegated Norway Maple**) ~ hardy, vigorous, deciduous tree with handsome green leaves with white edges.

Acer pseudoplatanus '**Worley**' (**Golden Sycamore**) ~ vigorous, deciduous tree with five-lobed leaves, at first soft yellow-green, then golden and later green.

Betula papyrifera (**Canoe Birch/Paper Birch/White Birch**) ~ hardy, deciduous tree with gleaming white bark which, on old trees, peels in large strips.

Gleditsia triacanthos '**Sunburst**' ~ hardy, deciduous, medium-sized tree with bright yellow leaves.

Robinia pseudoacacia '**Frisia**' (**Common Acacia/False Acacia**) ~ small to medium-sized deciduous tree with rich golden-yellow leaves.

TOO MANY COLOURS

Do not plant trees with differently coloured or striped bark in a group in a lawn, as this confuses the eye. A small group of *Betula pendula* (Silver Birch) is attractive, but if several *Acer davidii* (Snakebark Maple) were added the display would look confused.

STAKING TREES IN LAWNS

When supporting trees in lawns, use a vertical stake rather than an oblique or H-type, although these may be required later should the original stake decay.

Fragrant lawn trees

Several fragrant flowering trees are ideal for lawns:

***Malus coronaria* var. *dasycalyx* 'Charlottae' (Flowering Crab):** shell-pink, semi-double, violet-scented flowers in late spring and early summer.

***Prunus padus* 'Watereri' (Bird Cherry):** long, drooping tassels, packed with almond-scented white flowers during late spring and often into early summer.

***Prunus x yedoensis* (Yoshino Cherry):** white, almond-scented flowers during mid- to late spring.

Trees as focal points

When looking down a garden, the eye needs a point on which it can focus. If this is not present, the mind often becomes confused. In gardens which are divided into several parts, paths leading through arches help to guide the eye, but in larger areas a tree – or a small group of trees – positioned either centrally or to one side and towards the end of a garden soon captures the viewer's attention (see below for a range of suitable trees).

Does a garden need a focal point?

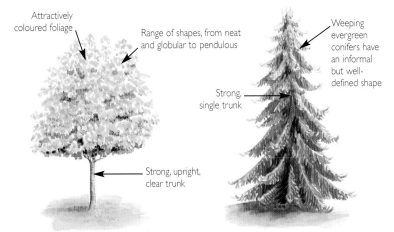

Deciduous tree

Attractively coloured foliage

Range of shapes, from neat and globular to pendulous

Strong, upright, clear trunk

Symmetrically shaped trees are usually positioned centrally rather than to one side.

Evergreen conifer

Weeping evergreen conifers have an informal but well-defined shape

Strong, single trunk

Evergreen conifers are often completely clothed in foliage, obscuring views beyond.

Trees that create focal points

***Acer platanoides* 'Drummondii' (Variegated Norway Maple)** ~ see opposite page for details.

***Betula pendula* (Silver Birch)** ~ hardy, deciduous tree with silvery bark. It has such a graceful nature that it is known as Lady of the Woods.

***Calocedrus decurrens* (Californian Incense Cedar/Incense Cedar)** ~ also known as *Libocedrus decurrens*, this hardy, slow-growing, evergreen conifer has a narrow, upright nature (see page 36 for details).

***Chamaecyparis lawsoniana* 'Lutea'** ~ hardy, evergreen conifer with a broad but columnar nature and golden-yellow foliage (see page 36 for details).

***Chamaecyparis lawsoniana* 'Winston Churchill'** ~ hardy, evergreen conifer with a broad but columnar habit and golden-yellow foliage (see page 37 for details).

***Cupressus sempervirens* (Italian Cypress/Mediterranean Cypress)** ~ hardy, evergreen conifer with an upright and columnar nature, and dark green foliage. It is ideal for introducing a Mediterranean atmosphere to a garden and looks at its best when in a small group (see page 37 for details).

***Larix decidua* (European Larch)** ~ hardy, slow-growing deciduous conifer with bright green foliage in spring (see page 37 for details).

***Picea breweriana* (Brewer's Weeping Spruce)** ~ hardy, evergreen conifer that has a weeping nature.

TYPE OF TREE THAT FORMS A FOCAL POINT

Both deciduous trees and conifers can be used to create focal points.

- **Deciduous trees** with coloured leaves attract attention even into late evening, while those with autumn-coloured foliage become beacons of interest when most other colour in a garden has ceased. Some trees, such as *Betula pendula* (Silver Birch), create greater impact when in a small group, while the spectacular *Liquidambar styraciflua* (Sweet Gum) is best when seen alone.
- **Evergreen conifers** create focal points through either their shape (such as the weeping *Picea breweriana*) or dramatically yellow-coloured foliage (*Chamaecyparis lawsoniana* 'Lutea' or *Chamaecyparis lawsoniana* 'Winston Churchill').
- **Deciduous conifers** are less dramatic, but few eyes would not be attracted by *Larix decidua* (European Larch) with its narrowly conic outline and bright green foliage in spring.

POSITIONING A FOCAL POINT

A tree when used as a focal point does not have to be close to a boundary. Indeed, never put a tree at risk from radical pruning because it later intrudes on neighbouring properties. Additionally, it does not have to be positioned centrally.

When choosing a position, look down the garden from the main viewing position – perhaps a patio or popular window that looks out onto the garden – and select a place that takes the eye, unobstructed, near to the end of your garden.

Shrubs & trees in small gardens

Do all shrubs and trees need to be small?

Shrubs and trees for small gardens are best selected for their small size or slow-growing nature (many are suggested on these pages). Yet it is also possible to use a few shrubs that you know will become too large and eventually have to be removed. If possible, a year or so before their removal use healthy stems as propagative material (see pages 70–71 for increasing shrubs and trees).

Brachyglottis 'Sunshine'

QUALITIES TO LOOK FOR

Small is beautiful: although small, a shrub or tree should have an attractive, natural appearance and not have to rely on being radically pruned each year – which does not work.

Slow-growing nature: avoid shrubs and trees that grow rapidly and soon outgrow their allotted position. Such plants are a waste of money, as too soon they have to be removed.

Varying interests: where possible, select a shrub or tree that has several qualities, such as flowers and handsome leaves, or beautiful bark and coloured leaves in autumn.

Easy to establish: rapid and easy establishment are essential, so always buy a healthy plant (for what to look for, see pages 8–9). Do not buy an inferior plant just because it is cheap.

Non-invasive: check that the plant is not invasive and will not soon dominate nearby plants or spread into neighbouring gardens. Hedging plants such as x *Cupressocyparis leylandii* (Leyland Cypress) are too vigorous.

SHRUBS FOR SMALL GARDENS

Berberis darwinii **(Darwin's Berberis):** hardy, evergreen shrub with deep yellow flowers in late spring. Small, prickly, holly-like leaves.

Brachyglottis **'Sunshine':** also known as *Senecio* 'Sunshine', an evergreen shrub with silvery-grey leaves and daisy-like, yellow flowers during early and mid-summer (illustrated on page 32).

Caryopteris x *clandonensis* **(Bluebeard):** relatively hardy deciduous shrub with aromatic, grey-green leaves and clusters of blue flowers during late summer and into autumn (illustrated on page 22).

Ceratostigma willmottianum **(Chinese Plumbago/Hardy Plumbago):** half-hardy deciduous shrub with small, blue flowers during mid- and late summer, and sometimes into autumn. Coloured leaves in autumn (illustrated on page 23).

Choisya ternata **(Mexican Orange Flower):** slightly tender evergreen shrub with sweetly scented white flowers mainly during mid- and late spring, but also intermittently throughout summer. The leaves, when bruised, emit a bouquet reminiscent of oranges (illustrated on page 20).

Cistus x *dansereaui* **(Rock Rose/Sun Rose):** evergreen shrub with white flowers splashed crimson during early and mid-summer. Attractive dark green leaves (illustrated on page 23).

Cytisus x *praecox* **(Warminster Broom):** hardy, deciduous shrub with creamy-white flowers in late spring and early summer.

Daphne mezereum **(February Daphne/Mezereon/Mezereum):** hardy, deciduous shrub with purple-red flowers from late winter to spring. These are borne on bare stems and followed by scarlet, poisonous berries (illustrated on page 18).

Forsythia x *intermedia* **(Golden Bells):** hardy, deciduous shrub with masses of golden-yellow flowers in early and mid-spring.

The leaves appear when flowering has finished (illustrated on page 20).

Fuchsia magellanica **(Lady's Eardrops):** slightly tender shrub with crimson and purple flowers from mid-summer to autumn.

Hebe **'Autumn Glory' (Shrubby Veronica):** hardy, evergreen shrub with deep purplish-blue flowers from mid-summer to autumn. Glossy-green leaves edged in red when young (illustrated on page 24).

Helichrysum italicum **(Curry Plant/White-leaf Everlasting):** evergreen shrub with narrow, silvery-grey, needle-like leaves that emit a bouquet reminiscent of curry. Additionally, during early and mid-summer it bears clusters of mustard-yellow flowers (illustrated on page 24).

Hypericum **'Hidcote' (Rose of Sharon/St John's Wort):** hardy, almost evergreen shrub with golden-yellow flowers from mid-summer to autumn (illustrated on page 25).

Magnolia stellata **(Star Magnolia):** hardy, slow-growing deciduous shrub with fragrant, star-shaped, white flowers during early and mid-spring (illustrated on page 21).

Potentilla fruticosa **(Shrubby Cinquefoil):** hardy, deciduous shrub with buttercup-yellow flowers from early to late summer (illustrated on page 26).

Salvia officinalis **'Icterina':** slightly tender, short-lived shrub with green-and-gold variegated leaves (illustrated on page 35).

Syringa meyeri: hardy, deciduous, small-leaved lilac with violet-purple flowers during early summer. Occasionally, there is a further flush of flowers (illustrated on page 26).

Weigela **hybrids:** hardy, deciduous shrubs with masses of flowers in early summer. Several superb forms (see page 27).

TREES FOR SMALL GARDENS

Acer griseum (**Paperbark Maple**): hardy, deciduous, slow-growing tree with coloured bark and mid-green leaves that assume rich scarlet and red shades in autumn (illustrated on page 30).

Acer pensylvanicum (**Moosewood/Snakebark Maple**): hardy, deciduous tree with attractively striped bark and pale to mid-green leaves that in autumn assume soft yellow shades (illustrated on page 30).

Amelanchier lamarckii (**June Berry/Shadbush/Snowy Mespilus**): hardy, deciduous shrub or small tree with pure white flowers during mid-spring. In autumn it has leaves that assume red and soft yellow shades (illustrated on page 20).

Betula albosinensis **var.** *septentrionalis*: hardy, deciduous tree with shiny, orange-brown bark with a grey and pink bloom. The mid-green leaves are covered in silky hairs.

Betula ermanii: hardy, deciduous tree with beautifully coloured bark – orange-brown and peeling to creamy-white. The leaves are attractive, but in cold areas are sometimes damaged by spring frosts.

Cercidiphyllum japonicum (**Katsura Tree**): hardy, deciduous tree with colourful leaves, both when they unfold in spring and in autumn when revealing rich tints. The tree also has the aroma of burnt sugar (illustrated on page 28).

Cercis siliquastrum (**Judas Tree/Love Tree**): hardy, deciduous tree or large shrub with rose-purple flowers in early summer. These are followed by attractive seed pods, tinted red when fully ripe in late summer.

Cornus florida (**Flowering Dogwood**): hardy, deciduous shrub or tree with dark green leaves that in autumn assume brilliant shades of scarlet and orange. Additionally, it has attractive flowers in late spring and early summer (illustrated on page 28).

Hamamelis mollis

Davidia involucrata (**Dove Tree/Handkerchief Tree**): hardy, deciduous tree with large, creamy-white bracts (modified leaves) during early summer.

Enkianthus campanulatus: hardy, deciduous tree with creamy-white, bell-shaped flowers with red veins. In autumn the leaves turn a brilliant red (illustrated on page 28).

Hamamelis mollis (**Chinese Witch Hazel**): hardy, deciduous shrub or small tree with sweetly scented, spider-like, golden-yellow flowers during early and mid-winter. Additionally, it has coloured leaves in autumn (illustrated on page 19).

Laburnum x *watereri* '**Vossii**' (**Golden Chain Tree/Golden Rain Tree**): hardy, deciduous tree with long, pendent, clusters of fragrant, yellow flowers in early summer (illustrated on page 25).

Magnolia sieboldii: hardy, deciduous shrub or small tree with white, bowl-shaped, fragrant flowers with conspicuous rosy-crimson or maroon stamens at their centres from early to late summer (illustrated on page 25).

Malus x *purpurea* '**Lemoinei**': hardy, deciduous tree with purple-crimson flowers during mid- and late spring. Additionally, the purple leaves assume bronze tinges in late summer and into autumn.

Prunus '**Accolade**': hardy, deciduous tree with a graceful appearance and clusters of blush-pink flowers during early and mid-spring).

Prunus serrula (**Birch-bark Tree**): hardy, deciduous tree with mahogany-like bark and slender-pointed, willow-like leaves. Additionally, it has white flowers in spring.

Syringa vulgaris (**Common Lilac**): hardy, deciduous shrub or small tree with fragrant flowers during late spring and early summer. There are many varieties, in colours including white, mauve, lavender-blue, soft-pink and deep purple.

SLOW-GROWING AND DWARF CONIFERS

Abies balsamea '**Hudsonia**': hardy, evergreen conifer with a slow-growing nature; it forms a flattish top with grey-green leaves that turn mid-green in mid-summer.

Juniperus communis '*Depressa Aurea*'

Cedrus deodara '**Golden Horizon**': slow-growing, evergreen conifer with a graceful then cascading habit.

Chamaecyparis lawsoniana '**Minima Aurea**': hardy, evergreen, dwarf and slow-growing conifer with golden-yellow foliage.

Chamaecyparis pisifera '**Filifera Aurea**': slow-growing, evergreen conifer with golden, thread-like foliage (see page 38).

Juniperus communis '**Depressa Aurea**': distinctive, hardy, evergreen conifer with bright yellow foliage in spring and summer, turning bronze in autumn (see page 39).

Juniperus scopulorum '**Skyrocket**': hardy, columnar, evergreen conifer with blue-grey foliage (see page 39).

Juniperus squamata '**Blue Star**': hardy, slow-growing, evergreen conifer with a spreading nature and silvery-blue, awl-shaped leaves.

Taxus baccata '**Standishii**': hardy, columnar, evergreen conifer with golden-yellow foliage (see page 39).

Large conifers

Chamaecyparis lawsoniana '**Columnaris Glauca**' ~ hardy, evergreen, narrow conifer, densely packed with glaucous, pale grey foliage (illustrated on page 36).

Chamaecyparis lawsoniana '**Pembury Blue**' ~ hardy, evergreen, conical conifer with silvery-blue foliage (illustrated on page 37).

Cupressus macrocarpa '**Goldcrest**' ~ hardy, evergreen conifer, initially narrow but later broadening, with rich yellow, feather foliage (illustrated on page 37).

Cupressus sempervirens (**Italian Cypress**) ~ slightly tender, evergreen, narrow and upright conifer with densely packed, dark green foliage (illustrated on page 37).

Colour throughout the year

Can I have colour throughout the year?

By selecting a range of flowering shrubs and trees – as well as foliage plants and those with colourful bark and berries – it is possible to have colour in your garden throughout the year. Most shrubs and trees flower during spring and summer, and a few in winter. Evergreen shrubs and trees produce displays all year round. Coloured bark can be seen throughout the year, and coloured stems during the winter months. Berries are mainly seen in autumn and winter.

SEASONAL AND YEAR-THROUGH COLOUR

FLOWERS	EVERGREENS	LEAVES	STEMS	BERRIES	BARK
Summer colour:	*For detailed information, see pages 32–35.*	*For detailed information, see pages 28–29.*	*For detailed information, see pages 30–31.*	*For detailed information, see pages 42–43.*	*For detailed information, see pages 30–31.*
Buddleja davidii (Butterfly Bush): range of colours, including violet-purple, blue, white and lilac.	**Aucuba japonica 'Variegata' (Spotted Laurel):** shiny, dark green leaves spotted and splashed in yellow.	**Cercidiphyllum japonicum (Katsura Tree):** rich green, red and yellow tints in autumn.	**Cornus alba (Dogwood):** rich red shoots in winter.	**Callicarpa bodinieri var. giraldii (Beauty-berry):** masses of dark lilac or pale violet berries.	**Acer griseum (Paperbark Maple):** buff-coloured bark peels to reveal orange-brown underbark.
Caryopteris x clandonensis (Bluebeard): blue.	**Brachyglottis 'Sunshine':** silvery-grey leaves with white-felted undersides.	**Cornus florida (Flowering Dogwood):** brilliant shades of scarlet and orange in autumn.	**Cornus alba 'Sibirica' (Westonbirt Dogwood):** brilliant crimson stems in winter.	**Chaenomeles speciosa (Cydonia/ Flowering Quince):** greenish-yellow fruits that last into winter.	**Acer pensylvanicum (Snakebark Maple):** mature trees with jagged white lines.
Genista hispanica (Spanish Gorse): deep yellow.	**Elaeagnus pungens 'Maculata' (Thorny Elaeagnus):** glossy-green leaves splashed with gold.	**Enkianthus campanulatus:** brilliant red tones in autumn.	**Cornus sericea 'Flaviramea' (Dogwood):** masses of bright, greenish-yellow stems during winter.	**Clerodendrum trichotomum (Glory-bower):** initially bright blue, later black, berries that persist into early winter.	**Arbutus x andrachnoides:** cinnamon-red bark that glows when in full sun.
Hebe 'Autumn Glory' (Shrubby Veronica): purplish-blue.	**Euonymus fortunei 'Emerald 'n' Gold':** masses of golden-variegated leaves that turn bronzy-pink in winter.	**Fothergilla major:** rich shades of red and orange-yellow in autumn.	**Rubus cockburnianus (Ornamental Bramble):** upright stems with a white, waxy bloom tinged blue. Especially attractive in winter.	**Cotoneaster lacteus:** clusters of red berries persist well into winter.	**Betula albosinensis var. septentrionalis:** shiny, orange-brown bark with a grey and pink bloom.
Hydrangea macrophylla (Common Hydrangea): from pink to blue.	**Fatsia japonica (False Castor Oil Plant):** large, glossy, hand-like green leaves.	**Liquidambar styraciflua (Sweet Gum):** leaves assume rich shades of crimson, purple and orange in autumn.		**Gaultheria mucronata:** white to pink, purple and red berries that persist through winter.	**Betula pendula (Silver Birch):** fine silvery bark.
Hypericum 'Hidcote' (Rose of Sharon): golden-yellow.	**Ilex aquifolium 'Madame Briot' (Variegated Holly):** spiny, green leaves mottled gold and light green.	**Parrotia persica:** shades of gold, amber and crimson in autumn.		**Malus x robusta 'Red Sentinel' (Ornamental Crab Apple):** bright, deep red berries that remain throughout winter.	**Betula utilis 'Jacquemontii':** dazzling white bark on the trunk and branches.
Laburnum x watereri 'Vossii' (Golden Chain Tree): golden-yellow.		**Rhus typhina (Stag's Horn Sumach):** rich shades of orange, red and purple in autumn.			**Prunus serrula (Birch-bark Tree):** bright, reddish-brown, peeling bark.
Philadelphus Hybrids (Mock Orange): white.					
Potentilla fruticosa (Shrubby Cinquefoil): yellow or red.					

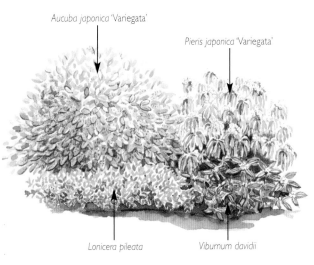

Aucuba japonica 'Variegata'

Pieris japonica 'Variegata'

Lonicera pileata

Viburnum davidii

Shrubs with variegated or interestingly shaped leaves create magnificent colour throughout the year.

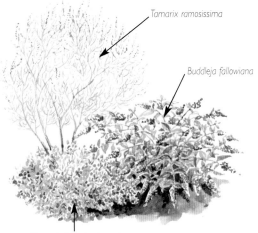

Tamarix ramosissima

Buddleja fallowiana

Caryopteris x clandonensis

Shrubs with colourful flowers always capture attention, and colour-harmonizing groups create further interest.

ATTRACTIVE COMBINATIONS OF SHRUBS AND TREES

Part of the art and excitement of growing shrubs and trees is to arrange them in attractive combinations. Creating harmonies and contrasts in shapes and colours will make your garden distinctive. In addition to the two associations of plants featured above, there are other combinations to consider. Some are associations of colour, others of attractive leaf textures and patterns.

COLOUR HARMONIES AND CONTRASTS FOR SMALL GARDENS

Many combinations of plants are simple and easy and do not involve vast expense and large numbers of plants. Yet they create more than double the pleasure of two separate plants.
Here are five associations of plants to try.
• Plant yellow, trumpet-faced daffodils in front of a small, internal hedge of *Lavandula angustifolia* 'Hidcote' (Lavender). It is hardy and evergreen, with narrow, silvery-grey leaves that create a superb background for the yellow daffodils. See page 47 for details of this shrub when planted as a hedge.

• Plant groups of the bulbous blue-flowered *Muscari armeniacum* (Grape Hyacinth) under the deciduous, spring-flowering *Magnolia stellata* (Star Magnolia), a shrub which produces a wealth of star-like, 10 cm (4 in) wide, white flowers during early and mid-spring. See page 21 for details of this shrub.
• Plant the hardy, evergreen, low-growing shrub *Erica carnea* 'King George', with rose-pink flowers during winter, in front of *Hamamelis mollis* (Chinese Witch Hazel). This shrub has sulphur-yellow, spider-like flowers during mid- and late winter. See page 19 for details of *Erica carnea*, and page 29 for *Hamamelis mollis* 'Pallida'.
• Plant the hardy, deciduous shrub *Magnolia liliiflora* 'Nigra', with 10 cm (4 in) long, chalice-shaped, reddish-purple flowers during mid-spring and into early summer, in front of a *Taxus baccata* (Yew) hedge. For details of the *Magnolia*, see page 21.
• Plant the bulbous *Fritillaria imperialis* (Crown Imperial), with clusters of reddish-orange flowers, around the *Syringa vulgaris* (Common Lilac), with flowers in a range of colours including white, mauve, lavender-blue, soft pink and deep purple. For details of this shrub, see page 27.

WINTER PATTERNS

Winter colour and interest need not only be created by flowers. Frost-covered stems and leaves also have eye appeal, especially when they glitter in low-angled rays of the sun. Additionally, if the shrub is in a 'mixed' border, the stems and leaves of herbaceous plants which have been left in place until spring will reflect sunlight.

FRAGRANT FLOWERS

Many shrubs featured in this book have fragrant flowers, including:

• *Chimonanthus praecox* (Winter Sweet) – page 18.
• *Choisya ternata* (Mexican Orange Blossom) – page 20.
• *Daphne mezereum* (Mezereum) – page 18.
• *Hamamelis mollis* (Chinese Witch Hazel) – page 19.

AROMATIC LEAVES

Many shrubs featured in this book have aromatic leaves, including:

• *Caryopteris* x *clandonensis* (Bluebeard) – page 22.
• *Cercidiphyllum japonicum* (Katsura Tree) – page 28.
• *Choisya ternata* (Mexican Orange Blossom) – page 20.
• *Choisya ternata* 'Sundance' (Yellow-leaved Mexican Orange Blossom) – page 33.

Mediterranean gardens

Can shrubs cope with hot weather?

Many shrubs grow well in hot climates, especially if they have aromatic or silvery leaves and are native to warm areas. It is possible to grow other shrubs in warm situations, but they need more attention and regular watering throughout summer, which can be impossible for many gardeners. Silvery leaves reflect hot rays from the sun, while aromatic leaves create a thin, insulative area above them. Many white-flowered shrubs are well suited to warm climates.

SHRUBS AND TREES FOR WARM AREAS

Many shrubs with aromatic, silvery, hairy or woolly leaves grow well in relatively dry soils in full sun, including the following.

Artemisia arborescens: deciduous or semi-evergreen tender shrub with silvery-white leaves and round, yellow flowers during early and mid-summer.

Brachyglottis '**Sunshine**' (also known as *Senecio* 'Sunshine'): see below.

Caryopteris x *clandonensis*: bushy, deciduous shrub with aromatic, grey-green leaves; also blue flowers during late summer and into autumn.

Hippophae rhamnoides (**Sea Buckthorn**): hardy, deciduous shrub with narrow, silvery leaves and bright orange berries during autumn and winter.

Perovskia atriplicifolia (**Russian Sage**): shrubby, with a herbaceous nature and grey-green leaves. It produces tall spires of violet-blue flowers in late summer and early autumn.

Phlomis fruticosa (**Jerusalem Sage**): shrubby and evergreen, with woolly, grey-green leaves and yellow flowers during early and mid-summer.

Romneya coulteri var. *trichocalyx* (**Californian Tree Poppy**): semi-woody, with blue-green leaves and white flowers from mid- to late summer.

SILVER- AND GREY-LEAVED SHRUBS

Brachyglottis 'Sunshine' *(also known as Senecio 'Sunshine') has attractive, silvery-grey leaves with white-felted undersides.*

Artemisia abrotanum *(Southernwood/Lad's Love) is a bushy shrub with a deciduous or semi-evergreen nature and sweetly aromatic, grey, downish leaves.*

Santolina chamaecyparissus *(Cotton Lavender) forms a mound of finely divided, silvery, woolly leaves. Bright yellow flowers appear in mid-summer.*

Agave americana 'Marginata' is spiky in form and looks superb when surrounded by small pebbles or gravel.

Perovskia atriplicifolia (Russian Sage) creates a dominant feature. Cut all stems to 30–45 cm (1–1½ ft) high in spring.

The art of topiary

Topiary was known to the Romans more than 2,000 years ago, when ships and hunting scenes were formed out of Cypress, with clipped **Box** used to spell names. Topiary became popular in Europe and was used formally to create spheres, squares and cones, as well as informally to depict animals. Both grand houses and cottage gardens enjoyed topiary. It is not difficult, but takes several years and regular clipping to produce an attractive feature.

What is topiary?

This upside-down hedge, formed by topiary techniques, creates an imaginative feature.

SUITABLE PLANTS

In Britain in the 1600s, plants such as Thrift, Hyssop, Lavender, Germander and Thyme were used for topiary, as well as more traditional woody plants like Box. Nowadays, many types of shrubs and trees, including conifers, are used and these embrace:
- *Buxus sempervirens* (Box)
- *Cupressus macrocarpa* (Monterey Cypress)
- *Cupressus sempervirens* (Italian Cypress)
- *Ilex aquifolium* (Holly)
- *Laurus nobilis* (Bay)
- *Lonicera nitida* (Chinese Honeysuckle)
- *Myrtus communis* (Myrtle)
- *Phillyrea angustifolia*

TOPIARY STYLE

A selection of formal (regular/geometric) shapes

A selection of informal (irregular/organic) shapes

CREATING A CONE

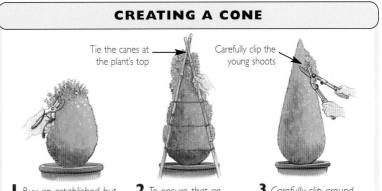

Tie the canes at the plant's top

Carefully clip the young shoots

1 *Buy an established but young* Buxus sempervirens *(Box) plant and, over a couple of seasons, carefully clip it to shape.*

2 *To ensure that an attractive cone will be created, position 3–4 long canes around the plant as shape guides.*

3 *Carefully clip around the cone. Remove the canes and trim the areas that earlier were cloaked by the canes. Always use sharp secateurs.*

CREATING A BIRD

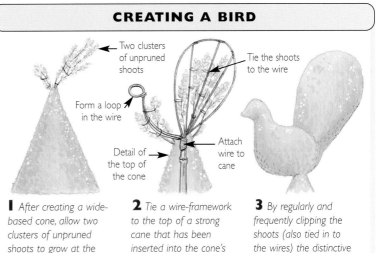

Two clusters of unpruned shoots

Tie the shoots to the wire

Form a loop in the wire

Detail of the top of the cone

Attach wire to cane

1 *After creating a wide-based cone, allow two clusters of unpruned shoots to grow at the top. Let them develop into long stems.*

2 *Tie a wire-framework to the top of a strong cane that has been inserted into the cone's centre. This will give shape guidance for the bird.*

3 *By regularly and frequently clipping the shoots (also tied in to the wires) the distinctive shape of a bird can eventually be created.*

Hedges for all gardens

Are hedges worth planting?

With open-plan front gardens, a boundary hedge is not a consideration, but for many people a hedge sets the tone of a property. Clinically trimmed foliage hedges indicate a neat and formal approach, whereas lax and informal hedges, perhaps with flowers, reflect a casual style. Gone are the days when *Ligustrum* (Privet) was solely used, and nowadays the range is wide – see pages 46–47 for examples, and pages 14–15 for how to plant a hedge.

FORMAL OR INFORMAL BOUNDARIES

Traditionally, formal hedges have been more popular than informal types, perhaps reflecting the need of many gardeners to create a defensive structure. Nowadays, however, informal and flowering hedges are becoming popular; the deciduous *Forsythia* x *intermedia* 'Spectabilis' creates a feast of yellow flowers in spring in town gardens, while the larger and evergreen *Berberis* x *stenophylla* is better for rural areas and where a thicker hedge is needed.

ARCHES IN HEDGES

Arches in boundary hedges are usually over paths and gates which give access to front doors. These arches are usually about 1.2 m (4 ft) wide; a gap greater than this is difficult to create and could be damaged by the weight of snow resting on top in a severe winter. Occasionally, circular and rectangular peephole gaps are clipped in boundary hedges, but these are difficult to create and maintain. Arches create mystique in a garden, and while *Taxus baccata* (Yew) has a formal appearance *Fagus sylvatica* (Beech) is deciduous and less strict and clinical; it also has the bonus of coloured leaves in autumn.

➔ *Neat, clinical arches can be created with* Taxus baccata *(Yew), a slow-growing evergreen conifer. Paths that are formed of gravel or old stone paving will harmonize with the Yew, which has an 'ancient' appearance.*

➔ *Arches with flattened tops initially need support from a framework of wood or wires. Wide arches are vulnerable to damage from heavy snowfalls.*
➔ *High-centred arches are dramatic and can introduce a Moorish feel to gardens. This one is formed from the slow-growing but densely foliaged Yew.*
➔ *Rounded arches that have a traditional English nature are easily created with Common Beech. This forms a strong arch that will withstand the rigours of winter.*

BAMBOO SCREENS

Screens formed of bamboos have a relaxed and informal look. Most bamboos which grow 1.8 m (6 ft) or more will create effective screens, and no pruning is needed. However, it is sometimes necessary to trim back shoots from spreading roots.

FLOWERING COASTAL HEDGES

Coastal gardens – or even those which are located several kilometres inland – often suffer from salt spray and strong, persistent winds, especially during winter. There are, however, several hedging shrubs that can be used (and in warm areas), including:

- *Escallonia rubra* var. *macrantha*: evergreen shrub, forming a hedge about 1.5–1.8 m (5–6 ft) high – sometimes more in warm areas. From early to late summer, it bears clusters of rose-red flowers. Space plants about 45 cm (18 in) apart. Another form, *Escallonia rubra* 'Crimson Spire', has an upright habit, with dark foliage and crimson flowers at the tips of its spire-like shoots. Because of its upright, non-bushy growth, position plants about 38 cm (15 in) apart. If *Escallonia* hedges need pruning, do this once a year and immediately the flowers fade. Do not prune severely, however, as this inhibits the development of flowers.
- *Fuchsia magellanica* (**Hardy Fuchsia**): bushy, slightly tender, deciduous shrub, which produces crimson and purple flowers from mid-summer to autumn (see also pages 14 and 47).
- *Olearia macrodonta* (**Daisy Bush**): evergreen shrub, not as hardy as *Olearia* x *haastii* but survives wind and salt spray in mild coastal areas. It has holly-like leaves and small, white daisy-like flowers in clusters up to 15 cm (6 in) across during early and mid-summer. The entire plant has a musk-like odour. Space plants 45 cm (18 in) apart.
- *Tamarix ramosissima* (**Tamarisk**): also known as *Tamarix pentandra*, this deciduous shrub has a lax habit and bears feathery, rose-pink flowers during late summer. It is ideal as a windbreak; space plants 60 cm (2 ft) apart and cut all stems to 30 cm (12 in) above the ground. Also, remove the tips of young shoots when they are 15 cm (6 in) long. This will create a bushy windbreak. Subsequently – and when the plants are established – in late winter cut all shoots to within 15 cm (6 in) of their base.

Low hedges, 75 cm (2½ ft) or less in height, can be formed by Miniature, Patio, Dwarf Polyantha and low-growing Floribunda Roses. They can be planted in a single row, with 30–38 cm (12–15 in) between them, but ensure that the foliage will overlap.

- **'Marlena':** superb Patio Rose, with masses of small, scarlet-crimson flowers over a long period. Height: about 38 cm (15 in).
- **'The Fairy':** graceful Polyantha Rose, with small, soft pink blooms. It is not the earliest to flower, but continues its display over a long period. Height: about 60 cm (2 ft).
- **'White Pet':** you might see this sold as 'Little White Pet'. It is a perpetual-flowering sport of 'Félicité Perpétue' and forms a bush with clusters of small, white, pompon-like flowers. Height: about 60 cm (2 ft).

Tall Rose hedge

Several Roses are suitable for creating a tall hedge, including 'Penelope' (illustrated right). It is a Hybrid Musk, with large trusses of fragrant, creamy-pink flowers. Later, it bears small, coral-pink hips (heps).

PEOPLE-PROOF ROSE HEDGES

As well as dense evergreen hedges, there are Roses that create stout, impenetrable hedges. These include:

Rosa **'Roseraie de l'Hay'**~ also known as *Rosa rugosa* 'Roseraie de l'Hay', this robust, prickly rose has large, double, crimson-mauve flowers mainly during early summer, with the bonus of round, orange-red hips (fruits) in early autumn. Space plants 45 cm (18 in) apart, in single or double rows.

Rosa **'Fruhlingsgold'**~ this is a Pimpinellifolia Hybrid of the Scots Briar, with a hardy and tough nature that forms an impenetrable barrier. It bears large, semi-double, fragrant, primrose-yellow flowers early in the season. The young shoots have red-gold prickles. Space plants 45–50 cm (18–20 in) apart.

Rosa **'Scabrosa'**~ also known as *Rosa rugosa* 'Scabrosa', this prickly-stemmed rose has large, single, rose-magenta flowers. They are followed in autumn by large, orange-red hips (fruits). Space plants 45 cm (18 in) apart, in single or double rows.

COLD AND EXPOSED COASTAL AREAS

If all other hedges fail because of persistent, cold wind, thorn trees will not let you down. They are robust, deciduous trees.

- *Crataegus monogyna* (**Common Hawthorn/Quick/May**): thorny, resilient tree with lobed, glossy, dark green leaves and clusters of white, heavily scented flowers during late spring. In autumn, it has crimson haws (fruits). For a dense hedge, space plants 30–38 cm (12–15 in) apart. After planting, cut all stems by half to encourage the development of branches at ground level.
- *Crataegus laevigata* (**Hawthorn/ May**): also known as *Crataegus oxyacantha*, this hardy, thorn-clad tree has shallowly lobed, mid-green leaves and sweetly scented white flowers during late spring. In autumn it has crimson haws (fruits). For a dense hedge, space plants 30 cm (12 in) apart. Immediately after planting, cut all stems by half to encourage the development of branches at ground level.

Pruning shrubs and trees

Do all shrubs and trees need pruning?

While many shrubs and trees need little pruning – other than the removal of dead flowers, cutting out twiggy growth and sawing off old branches – others need yearly pruning to encourage the regular development of good-quality flowers. Shrubs growing in temperate climates can be divided into three main flowering periods, which in turn influences the way they are pruned: 'winter', 'spring and early summer' and 'mid- and late summer'.

DO TREES NEED PRUNING?

Most ornamental trees need little pruning once they are planted, securely supported and after initial shaping. You should regularly check the tree throughout its life, especially in winter and after heavy snowfalls which may weigh down branches, perhaps causing them to break.

Deciduous trees: most trees should be pruned during their dormant period in the winter, but Ornamental Cherry trees and other members of the *Prunus* family are best pruned in late spring or early summer, when their sap is beginning to rise. This ensures that disease spores will be less likely to gain entry to the tree and to infect it.

Evergreen trees: cut out any misplaced branches when the tree is young in order to create a balanced shape for the tree, but make sure that there is only one leading shoot. This is best done in spring.

Pruning evergreen shrubs

These are clothed in leaves throughout the year, with new ones being formed and old ones falling off. The usual reasons for pruning are to create shapely plants and to prevent them crowding their neighbours. Do not prune in winter; mid- or late spring is best, just when growth is beginning. However, if the shrub is flowering, defer pruning until they fade. Some variegated shrubs produce shoots that have reverted to all green. Cut these back to their point of origin as soon as they are noticed.

PRUNING DECIDUOUS SHRUBS

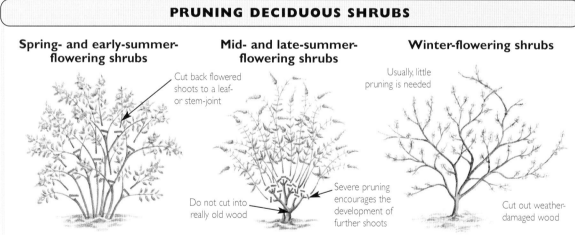

Spring- and early-summer-flowering shrubs

Cut back flowered shoots to a leaf- or stem-joint

Mid- and late-summer-flowering shrubs

Do not cut into really old wood

Severe pruning encourages the development of further shoots

Winter-flowering shrubs

Usually, little pruning is needed

Cut out weather-damaged wood

↗ Early-flowering shrubs – flowering from spring to the later part of early summer – bear flowers on shoots produced during the previous year. These encompass shrubs such as *Forsythia*, *Ribes* (Flowering Currants), *Philadelphus* (Mock Orange), *Deutzia* and *Weigela*. Prune these shrubs immediately their flowers fade, cutting back flowered shoots to young, strong growths. Also, cut out dead, crossing and congested shoots.

↗ These shrubs flower from mid-summer through to autumn and include *Buddleja davidii* (Butterfly Bush), *Caryopteris*, *Potentilla* and *Hibiscus*. Because they flower too late in the year to produce shoots that would ripen and be hardy during winter, they are left alone until the following spring. Some of them need little pruning, other than the removal of dead and twiggy growths, but *Buddleja davidii* is best cut hard back in spring.

↗ Winter-flowering deciduous shrubs need little pruning. When they are young, prune them to create an attractive shape. Later in their lives – as soon as their flowering display is over – cut out any congested stems and those that have become diseased or damaged by severe weather. If these are left, they will encourage decay to infect and damage other parts of the shrub. Keep the shrub's centre open so that light and air can enter.

TRIMMING HEATHERS AND ERICAS

Keep these tidy by lightly trimming with hedging shears (secateurs do not enable contoured outlines to be created).

Callunas and summer-flowering Ericas: trim in spring, before new growth appears; lightly clip off dead flowers.

Winter- and spring-flowering Ericas: trim after the flowers fade, cutting off dead flowerheads.

Daboecias: cut off old flowerheads and loose ends of shoots in late autumn, after flowering has finished. In cold areas, you should leave this job until spring.

PRUNING TOOLS

Secateurs

There are two types of secateurs:
- **Bypass:** also known as parrot-type secateurs, these have a cutting action in which two blades overlap and cross each other, producing a surgical cut.
- **Anvil:** to cut, one blade meets a fixed, firm surface known as the anvil. These are widely used by professional gardeners. Most secateurs suit right-handed gardeners, but left-handed types are also available.

Long-handled loppers

These resemble secateurs, but with long handles. Those with handles 38–45 cm (15–18 in) long cut shoots up to 36 mm (1½ in) thick, while heavy-duty types, with handles 75 cm (2½ ft) long, sever stems 5 cm (2 in) thick. Some loppers have a compound cutting action that enables thick shoots to be cut with greater ease and accuracy.

Pruning saws

These are good for cutting branches and thick stems. Grecian saws (with a curved, tapering blade that cuts on the pull stroke) are ideal for cutting awkwardly positioned branches. Other saws have coarse teeth and are better for thick branches. Depending on their size, saws will cut wood up to 18 cm (7 in) thick – or even thicker in the case of bow saws.

Pruning knives

These sharp knives are used to smooth surfaces where large branches have been cut off with a saw (see above). Then coat the surface with a fungicidal wound paint.

PRUNING SHRUBS GROWN FOR THEIR COLOURED STEMS

Several Dogwoods (see pages 30–31) are grown for their coloured stems, which are especially welcome in winter when they are free from leaves and caught by low rays of the sun. Unless these shrubs are severely pruned in spring, by cutting all stems to within 7.5 cm (3 in) of the ground, they will not produce a good display of shoots during the following winter.

Stems produced the previous year

Do not cut into really old wood

PRUNING A WEIGELA

Weigelas are deciduous shrubs that flower during the latter part of late spring and into early summer; they need to be pruned immediately their flowers fade. This gives a shrub the longest possible period to develop and ripen young growth before the onset of cold, winter weather. These new shoots will bear flowers during the following season.

Cut out flowered stems

Remove twiggy shoots

1 *Use sharp secateurs to cut out all shoots that produced flowers. Flowered stems are easily identified as they are congested with dead flowers. Cut the complete stem back to young, strong shoots.*

2 *Cut out twiggy as well as crossing shoots. If left, they look unsightly and absorb some of the shrub's energy. They also prevent a good circulation of air within the shrub that otherwise would help to ripen young shoots.*

Renovating a neglected Weigela

A Weigela that has been neglected for several years will have few flowers and be congested with shoots of all ages. In early summer, cut out all old shoots (as well as those that have just produced flowers) to the shrub's base or main stems. This will encourage the development of fresh shoots that will bear flowers the following year.

Caring for hedges

Does a hedge need regular care?

Hedges are often the most neglected features in a garden. They will benefit from attention throughout their lives, however, especially when young. Newly planted deciduous hedges must be radically pruned to encourage a base that is packed with stems and leaves. Later, rounding or sloping the top of a hedge can help it survive heavy snowfalls. Here are a few clues to producing an eye-catching hedge, as well as rejuvenating evergreen hedges.

WALL OR HEDGE?

Hedges have both advantages and disadvantages over walls. Hedges are living parts of a garden and create superb boundaries as well as attractive backdrops for other plants. The choice of hedges is wide, with a range of heights and leaf colours. Some also produce flowers. Hedges are cheaper than walls and less likely to be damaged by severe wind or subsidence on clay soils, but it takes longer to produce a dense, leafy screen and regular attention will be needed throughout the year. Additionally, soil beneath and near to a hedge becomes deprived of moisture and plant foods.

HEDGE SHAPES

Round-topped
➔ Where winter weather is severe and snowfalls routine, clip the top of a hedge to either a round or shallowly tent-like outline. This will make it easy to dust or brush off snow.

Flat-topped
➔ Choose the shape of a hedge's top with care. In areas where heavy snowfalls are only a memory, a flat-topped or castellated hedge looks smart, especially in a formal garden.

PRUNING A DECIDUOUS HEDGE

| 1st YEAR | 2nd YEAR | 3rd YEAR |

1 To encourage the development of shoots and leaves from a hedge's base, it is essential that it is radically pruned when newly planted and during its first few years. Even though it may appear severe, cut back all shoots on a newly planted hedge by a half to two-thirds.

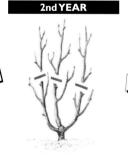

2 During the following year, cut back all new shoots by a half to two-thirds. This will encourage the development of young shoots that will form the foundation for other shoots that eventually will clothe the sides of the hedge. Creating an attractive hedge is not rapid – but it is necessary.

3 During the following year, cut the new stems back by one-third. In the following year – and all subsequent years – trim back all shoots by about the same amount. Regularly clipping an established hedge will create further shoots – and a mass of leaves.

Cut small-leaved hedges with hand shears or powered cutters.

LARGE-LEAVED HEDGES

When pruning large-leaved, informal, evergreen hedges, use neither hand shears nor electrical hedge-cutters. Both of these mince leaves and create an unsightly hedge. Instead, use sharp secateurs to cut the stems individually. Keep the blades clean and oiled to ensure they open and close easily. Do not leave long, bare stubs, as they decay back to a leaf-joint and look unsightly.

Cut each stem individually, 3–6 mm (⅛–¼ in) above a leaf.

RENOVATING OLD EVERGREEN HEDGES

Some hedges respond well to severe pruning and within a season or two are rejuvenated and attractive.

- *Aucuba japonica* '**Variegata**' **(Spotted Laurel/Gold Dust):** large and overgrown hedges can be cut back to about 60 cm (2 ft) high in spring. Although a radically pruned hedge looks unsightly, it will soon develop fresh, young shoots.
- *Buxus sempervirens* **(Box):** if hedges become too large, they can be cut back to old wood during mid- or late spring.
- *Ilex aquifolium* **(Holly):** where hedges have been neglected, they can be cut hard back in spring. Fresh shoots will develop from the hedge's base.
- *Ligustrum ovalifolium* **(Privet):** many Privet hedges outgrow their positions and radical pruning is needed. During late spring, cut back branches, reducing the height and width. The yellow-leaved form can be treated in a similar way, but not so radically.
- *Lonicera nitida* **(Chinese Honeysuckle):** overgrown and spreading hedges do not respond as well as Privet to severe pruning, especially when old. If light clipping does not create a better-looking hedge, consider digging it up and replacing it.

Safety first when using electrical clippers

When using electrical hedge-cutters, take care as both cables and fingers can easily be cut.

- Ensure that a circuit-breaker is fitted into the circuit.
- Wear and button up a stout jacket – do not wear a scarf or tie.
- Trail the lead over a shoulder.
- Wear protective goggles if the hedge is dusty.
- Keep all animals and children indoors.

RENOVATING AN OLD DECIDUOUS HEDGE

Neglected and old deciduous hedges, such as those formed of *Fagus sylvatica* (Beech), can be cut hard back in late winter. As long as the hedge is growing strongly, it soon recovers and produces a fresh covering of shoots and leaves. Later, resume clipping the hedge in summer. These pictures show end views of a neglected hedge (near right) and a radically pruned hedge (far right).

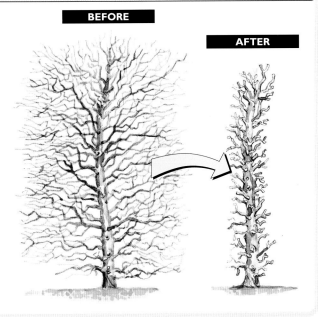

BEFORE

AFTER

BRUSHING OFF SNOW

Carefully brush snow off hedges, preferably before it freezes. This applies both to closely clipped and informal hedges, which can become just as distorted and flattened. Tapping branches removes a light dusting; a soft brush is better for thick coverings.

Increasing shrubs and trees

Is it easy to increase shrubs?

Some shrubs are easy to propagate, although it may take a year or so before a rooted plant is created and perhaps another season while it grows in a nursery bed until it is large enough to be planted out in a border. Nevertheless, few gardening activities can compare with the excitement of raising a few new plants yourself. The simplest way to increase a shrub is to layer a stem so that, where it touches the ground, it develops a new root system of its own.

LAYERING A SHRUB

1 Select a healthy, low-growing shoot, up to two years old. Lower it to the ground and form a shallow trench that slopes to 7.5–15 cm (3–6 in) deep at its lowest point, 23–45 cm (9–18 in) from the shoot's tip.

2 Lower the shoot into the depression and bend it upright. Wound the stem on the underside of the bend, either by making a tongued cut or cutting halfway around the stem and removing part of the bark.

3 Sprinkle sharp sand in the trench and use a forked stick or a bent piece of strong wire to hold the shoot in place. Also insert a strong, short cane into the compost, near to the shoot.

4 Draw friable soil over and around the shoot and firm it. Level the soil and tie the shoot to the cane, giving support but not strangling it. Add a dated label and thoroughly water the soil.

SHRUBS AND TREES THAT CAN BE LAYERED

- Amelanchier
- Azaleas
- Calluna
- Camellia
- Chaenomeles
- Cornus
- Cotinus
- Cotoneaster
- Daboecia
- Erica
- Euonymus
- Forsythia
- Garrya elliptica
- Hamamelis
- Jasminum nudiflorum
- Magnolia
- Pieris
- Piptanthus
- Rhododendron
- Rhus
- Stachyurus
- Vaccinium
- Viburnum
- Wisteria

How long before roots form?

After creating a layer, keep the surrounding area free from weeds. Also, during summer ensure that the soil remains moist, but not waterlogged. An indication that roots have formed is when fresh growth develops from the shoot's top. At this stage, carefully remove some of the soil and if roots are well developed untie the stem, remove the peg or bent wire and sever the original stem that joined the young plant to its parent. Transfer the new plant to a nursery bed, for later moving to its permanent position.

When to layer shrubs and trees

Shrubs and trees can be layered throughout the year, but late summer and early autumn, as well as spring, are best. Essentially, shoots must be sufficiently pliable to be lowered to the ground and then bent into the correct position.

HARDWOOD CUTTINGS

— Sharp sand

I In autumn, when plants are dormant and leafless, hardwood cuttings can be taken from mature shoots of the current season's growth. Cuttings are 23–38 cm (9–15 in) long and will take up to a year to form roots.

2 Remove the lower leaves and trim the cutting's base below a leaf-joint. Most plants increased by hardwood cuttings are deciduous, but some, like the Privet seen here, are evergreen or partially evergreen.

3 Use a spade to form a V-shaped trench, with one vertical side. Sprinkle sharp sand in the base and insert each cutting – a half to two-thirds of its length deep and about 10 cm (4 in) apart. Replace and firm the soil.

SHRUBS THAT CAN BE RAISED BY HARDWOOD CUTTINGS

• *Buddleja* • *Cornus alba* • *Cornus sericea (Cornus stolonifera)* • *Cotoneaster x watereri* • *Deutzia* • *Forsythia* • *Ligustrum ovalifolium* • *Philadelphus* • *Ribes* • *Rubus* • *Salix* • *Sambucus* • *Spiraea* • *Symphoricarpos* • *Tamarix* • *Viburnum* (deciduous types) • *Weigela*

How long before roots form?

Hardwood cuttings are taken in autumn, mainly from deciduous shrubs but sometimes from evergreens. If deciduous, wait until leaves fall from the shrub. After insertion (see above), they take about a year to form roots when inserted in open ground. In autumn, carefully dig them up and plant into a nursery bed or direct into a border. Alternatively, they can be inserted in pots and placed in a cold frame, when they usually have produced roots by late spring. First acclimatize them to garden conditions, and then plant them into a border or transfer them to pots, for later planting.

HALF-RIPE CUTTINGS

I Take half-ripe cuttings when shoots are firmer than for softwood types, but less mature than hardwood cuttings. Remove 10–15 cm (4–6 in) long shoots, preferably with a small piece of the older wood still attached to their bases.

2 Remove the lower leaves and trim the cutting's base, cutting off whisker-like growths around the older piece of wood (known as a heel). Not all half-ripe cuttings have heels, but when present they encourage rapid rooting.

3 Dip the base of each cutting in a hormone rooting-powder and insert them 3.5–5 cm (1½–2 in) deep in pots of equal parts of moist peat and sharp sand. Position each cutting 12–18 mm (½–¾ in) from the pot's edge. Firm and water the compost.

SHRUBS THAT CAN BE RAISED FROM HALF-RIPE CUTTINGS

• *Arctostaphylos* • *Aucuba* • *Berberis* • *Brachyglottis* • *Bupleurum* • *Callistemon* • *Camellia* • *Carpenteria* • *Ceanothus* (some) • *Cotoneaster* • *Cytisus* (some) • *Deutzia* • *Elaeagnus* • *Garrya elliptica* • *Ilex* (some) • *Lavandula* (some) • *Mahonia* • *Olearia* (some) • *Philadelphus* • *Pieris* • *Pyracantha* • *Viburnum* • *Weigela*

When to take half-ripe cuttings

Also known as semi-ripe cuttings, these are taken from a parent plant in mid- and late summer. The wood needs to be firm, but less mature than for hardwood cuttings.

How long before roots form?

Place the cuttings in pots in a sun-sheltered cold frame or under a cloche. Alternatively, they may produce roots when placed against a warm but sunless wall. Regularly check that the compost is evenly moist. By the following spring, cuttings usually have roots and can be planted into a nursery bed in a sheltered, lightly shaded corner of a garden. Ensure that the soil does not dry out. Later, move plants to their growing positions.

BUDDING AND GRAFTING

Budding and grafting involve uniting the growing part of a desired variety with a rootstock of known and desired vigour. Many Roses are increased by the budding method, and fruit trees such as apples by grafting.

Renovating shrubs and trees

Is shrub and tree renovation quick?

If a shrub has been neglected for only a few years, renovation and return to its former beauty is rapid. If a tree is covered in lichen and sporting a mass of water shoots, again renovation can soon be accomplished. If pruning a shrub means cutting into old wood, however, it can often take several years for it to regain a handsome canopy of leaves or display of flowers. For this reason, many gardeners prefer to dig up a neglected shrub and replace it.

REJUVENATING OLD TREES

Because ornamental trees need little regular pruning, even after several years of neglect they are easy to renovate. Some deciduous trees become covered with unsightly moss and lichen; spraying with a fruit tree winter-wash when the tree is dormant soon removes them. Water shoots appear on some neglected trees and their removal is described on page 74.

Tackling neglected fruit trees

Neglected apple and pear trees have masses of crossing branches and undersized fruits. Also, the tree is probably riddled with pests and diseases. Cut out cankered branches. There is then a judgement to make as to whether the amount of the tree that remains is worth saving; remember that renovation will take several years.

If the tree is worth keeping, during the first dormant season cut out all dead and diseased wood, as well as congested branches and shoots at the tree's centre. During the following year, cut back any excessively old branches, and in the following dormant season start pruning the smaller shoots. Spray the tree regularly and feed the soil around its base.

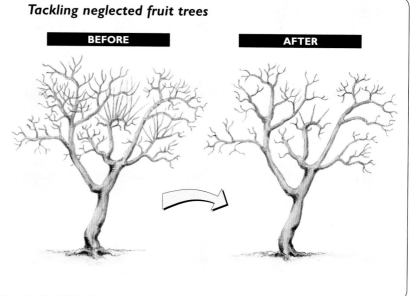

BEFORE

AFTER

NEGLECTED ORNAMENTAL TREES

Large trees – perhaps an aged, prized and distinctive oak, for example – sometimes develop cavities that if not 'doctored' would spread and result in having to cut down the tree. Squirrels and some birds may damage the bark, with deterioration spreading and creating a cavity. The treatment needed depends on the depth of the damage.

- **Shallow damage, and mainly to the bark:** cut away all the damaged bark, trim the edges of the wound with a sharp knife and coat it with a fungicidal paint.

- **Shallow cavities:** scrape away all dead wood and remove debris that might have collected in the hole. Paint the entire surface with a fungicidal paint. Keeping the area open to the air is better than packing the hole with a filler that hardens, later shrinks and creates gaps for water to enter and cause further deterioration.

- **Deep cavities:** scrape away all dead wood and ensure that water can drain away. Seek advice from a tree surgeon about plugging the hole or cutting off the branch.

TIMING OF RENOVATION

You should plan to renovate deciduous trees during the winter, when they are dormant. However, do not prune flowering Cherry trees – or any *Prunus* species – in winter. Instead, you should wait until late spring or early summer when their sap is rising. Also wait until spring to severely prune evergreen shrubs. If these are pruned in late summer or early autumn, new shoots that quickly develop would be damaged by frost. By pruning in spring, the new young shoots will have all summer to ripen and will therefore be able to withstand the cold weather when it arrives.

ASSESSING NEGLECTED SHRUBS

Before grubbing out an old and neglected shrub, consider its replacement. A fresh, young shrub may take a year or more to become established and to fill its allotted space, whereas an established shrub can sometimes be rejuvenated within a year. Here is a *Hydrangea macrophylla* (Common Hydrangea) that has been neglected, forming a mass of old, tangled, crossing stems.

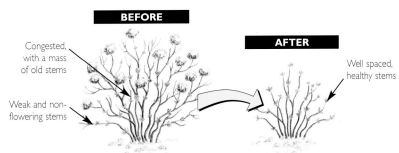

BEFORE

Congested, with a mass of old stems

Weak and non-flowering stems

AFTER

Well spaced, healthy stems

A TO Z OF SHRUB RENOVATION

Many shrubs, after a few years and especially if they have been neglected and left unpruned, need to be renovated. Here are a few popular shrubs that can be encouraged to return to their former glory.

Aucuba japonica 'Variegata'
Gold-dust Tree/Spotted Laurel
Cut back any large, overgrown shrubs during spring, to about 60 cm (2 ft) high. New stems will develop from the base of the shrub, although the plant may look rather unsightly for the first year after renovation.

Buddleja davidii
Butterfly Bush
This shrub is usually pruned every spring, cutting back stems to near their points of origin. If pruning is neglected, the shrub becomes a tangle of gnarled, old stems. Therefore, in spring cut all the stems back to within a few centimetres of the previous season's growth.

Camellia
Shrubs with old, bare stems and bases can be induced to produce further shoots by cutting them back by one-third to a half of their height in mid-spring.

Choisya ternata
Mexican Orange Blossom
Old shrubs with bare stems and bases benefit from having all their stems cut back in late spring. This will mean the loss of flowers for a year, but by the second year after renovation the shrub will look much more attractive.

Laurus nobilis
Bay
This evergreen shrub often becomes congested, overgrown and unattractive. Prune in mid-spring, cutting hard into old wood.

Prunus laurocerasus
Cherry Laurel
During early and mid-spring, cut stems and branches hard back into old wood. The shrub will appear unsightly for a couple of years following renovation pruning, but will then regain its handsome appearance.

Rhododendrons
With age, many species and hybrid Rhododendrons tend to become rather leggy and neglected. In such cases, they will respond well to being cut hard back to old wood in mid-spring. However, you should never prune grafted types or those with peeling bark – such as *Rhododendron barbatum* and *Rhododendron thomsonii* – in this way.

Roses – species types
These Roses usually need very little attention, and routine pruning consists of cutting out any weak, twiggy and congested shoots. However, any badly neglected shrubs that have unattractive bare stems can be cut back to 30–60 cm (1–2 ft) high in early spring. This will mean sacrificing flowers for a year or so, but will be worth the effort in the end.

Syringa vulgaris
Common Lilac
Neglected shrubs become unsightly, but they can be rejuvenated by cutting the entire plant back to 60–90 cm (2–3 ft) high in mid-spring. However, after such drastic treatment, it will then take several years for the shrub to produce flowers once again.

PROPAGATIVE MATERIAL

Before grubbing out a shrub, check whether shoots and stems can be used to increase the plant. Increasing plants by hardwood and half-ripe cuttings (also known as semi-ripe cuttings) is described on page 71.

GETTING NAILED!

Does knocking an iron nail into a fruit tree encourage it to bear fruit? Very little, if at all. It was earlier done under the premise that added iron would make up for any deficiency of iron in the soil.

Can a tree be killed by knocking a copper nail into it? This is a popular fallacy and is totally inaccurate. Although excessive copper is poisonous to plants, earlier it was a main ingredient of many fungicidal sprays and fortunately is not, in low concentrations, poisonous to trees.

Routine care of shrubs and trees

Are shrubs and trees self-reliant?

Apart from pruning shrubs and trees (see pages 66–67) and checking that trees are securely staked – especially in their early years – these plants will usually need little attention. However, other regular care is beneficial, including mulching, removing dead flowers and protecting young plants from strong, cold wind. Rabbit and squirrel damage (see page 77) is likely in rural areas and plastic tree-guards installed at planting time prevents bark being gnawed.

MULCHING AND WATERING

As well as providing plants with food, a mulch helps to suppress the growth of weeds. It also keeps the soil moist and cool during summer. In spring, use a garden fork to shallowly disturb the soil, breaking up crusty surfaces and removing weeds. Ensure roots of perennial weeds are completely removed. At this stage, parts of the mulch from the previous year may still be present and this can be lightly forked into the soil. Thoroughly soak the soil and apply a 7.5–10 cm (3–4 in) thick mulch of well-decomposed garden compost or manure. Leave a 7.5 cm (3 in) gap between the stems and mulch. Other mulching materials include bark chippings.

REMOVING WATER SHOOTS

Often, thin shoots (known as water shoots and occasionally as water sprouts and branch suckers) grow from a trunk and lower branches, especially on neglected lilacs. Use a Grecian saw to remove them and, if necessary, a sharp knife to ensure that the cuts are flush with the trunk. Some trees when neglected, such as the deep purple-leaved *Prunus cerasifera* 'Pissardii', produce masses of thin, somewhat twiggy stems. Again, use a saw to remove them close to the trunk or branches.

Saw off any water shoots as close as possible to the trunk of the tree as soon as you notice them.

Removing suckers

A sucker is a shoot that grows from below ground level and originates from a plant's roots or an underground stem. Sometimes, they are used to increase a plant. However, to most gardeners a sucker is a shoot that grows on a grafted or budded plant and develops from below the union.

Established shrub

Sucker shoot

Remove soil and pull off sucker

Suckers are mainly associated with budded or grafted Rose bushes and, if nothing is done about them, soon dominate the plant. Immediately a sucker is seen, use a trowel to remove soil from around its base. Then, instead of cutting it off – which encourages the development of further suckers – pull it off. Replace and firm soil around the stem.

REMOVING DEAD FLOWERS

Shrubs such as Rhododendrons that produce large flowers benefit from having old ones removed. As well as improving a shrub's appearance, 'deadheading' prevents the development of seeds and thereby directs all the plant's energies into growth. Hold the stem firm and snap the old flowerhead sideways. Place dead flowers on a compost heap.

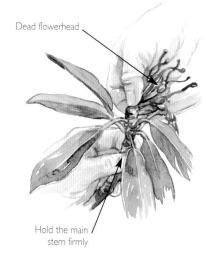

Dead flowerhead

Hold the main stem firmly

REMOVING A BRANCH

Occasionally, a large branch needs to be removed. In most cases, this is best tackled in winter, but choose late spring or early summer for ornamental Cherry trees. Cutting off a large branch is often a two-person task, especially if it means using a ladder, which must be in good condition and firmly positioned. A Grecian saw is ideal for cutting close to a branch in an awkward position.

LADDER STABILITY

A Grecian saw is ideal for home gardeners to use when standing on a ladder to cut a branch. This saw cuts on the pull stroke and therefore does not mean that the pruner is pushing away from the tree and perhaps dislodging the ladder.

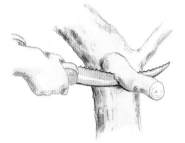

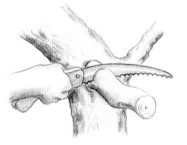

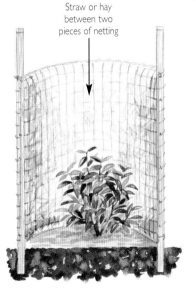

1 *Cut off the end part of the branch, 45–60 cm (1½–2 ft) from its point of origin. Take care that when it falls it does not collapse on top of the ladder – or you or a helper. Then, use a sharp saw to cut half to two-thirds of the way through the underside of the branch and close to the trunk.*

2 *Complete the cut by sawing from the upper side of the branch.*

3 *Use a sharp knife to pare the surface of the cut and its edges. When smooth, paint the surface and top edges with a fungicidal tree paint to prevent the entry of disease spores.*

PROTECTING NEWLY PLANTED SHRUBS FROM COLD WIND

Until established, newly planted shrubs – especially young and tender evergreens – are at risk of damage from cold and blustery wind. A protective screen for the windward side of a shrub can be quickly made from a sandwich of plastic-coated wire-netting and straw or hay.

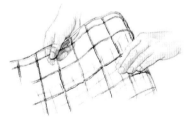

1 *Cut a 3–3.6 m (10–12 ft) long and 90 cm–1.2 m (3–4 ft) wide piece of wire-netting. Fold it in half.*

Straw or hay between two pieces of netting

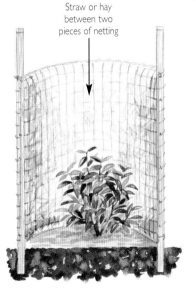

2 *Pack straw or hay between the two pieces of wire-netting.*

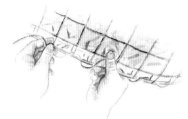

3 *Weave wire or stout string along the edges to hold them closed.*

4 *Form the screen into a half-circle and secure it to two strong posts.*

Pests and diseases

Are pests and diseases a major problem?

It is mainly the soft parts of trees and shrubs – such as flowers, young leaves and shoots – that are vulnerable to pests and diseases. Two of the most pernicious diseases are peach leaf curl and silver leaf (see below). Additionally, there are perennial problems from hungry birds, rabbits and squirrels, mainly during the winter season when food is scarce. Preventative measures such as tree-guards are essential, especially for people living in rural areas.

PESTS AND DISEASES AND HOW TO DEAL WITH THEM

Problem	Course of action
Caterpillars	Caterpillars are the larvae of moths and butterflies. They infest garden plants, eating and chewing their way through soft stems, flowers and leaves. The adults are harmless in themselves and gardeners often delight in seeing them. **What to do** Pick off small clusters of caterpillars. Alternatively, spray with a proprietary insecticide as soon as they – or the damage – is seen.
Cockchafers	Commonly known as May Bugs and June Bugs, both adult beetles and larvae attack plants. Adult beetles feed and fly during early and mid-summer, chewing flowers and leaves of many ornamental plants. The dirty, creamy-white larvae are about 30 mm (1¼ in) long and usually curled up. They live in the soil and chew roots. **What to do** Whenever possible, pick off and destroy adults and larvae. Additionally, dust leaves with an insecticide.
Greenfly	Also known as aphids and aphis, these sap-sucking pests mainly infest flowers, soft leaves and shoot tips. They suck sap, causing debilitation and spreading viruses. At the same time, they excrete honeydew, which attracts ants and encourages the presence of sooty mould, a black and unsightly fungus. **What to do** Spray shrubs with an insecticide as soon as damage or pests are seen.
Azalea gall	Although not a serious problem, azalea galls infect both pot-grown and outdoor azaleas and rhododendrons. It causes reddish swellings on leaves, quickly becoming covered with a greyish-white bloom. **What to do** If the infection is limited, pick off and burn the galls before they turn white. Usually, however, spraying is needed; use a proprietary spray.
Peach leaf curl	A fungal disease that infects almonds, apricots, nectarines and peaches, as well as ornamental trees related to them. Infected leaves are first seen in spring, soon after unfolding, with pale greenish-yellow areas. Later they assume deep crimson shading; leaves thicken and become coated in a white bloom. Leaves eventually fall off. **What to do** Spray with a proprietary fungicide in late winter, early spring and just before leaves fall in autumn.
Silver leaf	Mainly a problem of apricots, cherries, nectarines, peaches and Ornamental Cherries, this is a fungal disease that enters a tree through a wound or pruning cut. Branches become infected, producing silvered leaves and brown staining on infected wood. Shoots eventually die back. **What to do** Prune only when the sap is rising, and paint cuts with a fungicidal paint. Feeding aids partial recovery.

OTHER PROBLEMS

Problem	Course of action
Birds eating buds	Birds do most damage to buds. Specifically, blackbirds and tits damage fruits and flowers, bullfinches eat flower buds on tree fruits, soft fruits and ornamental trees and shrubs. Woodpeckers are often claimed to damage healthy trees, but usually they confine themselves to rotten or semi-decayed trees. **What to do** Fruit trees can be protected by cages, but ornamental trees and shrubs are invariably left unprotected.
Rabbits chewing trunks	To many people these are cuddly, furry fellows, but to gardeners they are some of 'nature's nasties'. They chew and scratch bark on trunks and woody stems, as well as eating soft shoots. **What to do** Fit plastic tree-guards to any newly planted trees, as well as other trees in vulnerable areas, especially in severe winters when other sources of food are scarce.
Squirrels chewing bark	Known to some people as 'tree-rats', they chew and strip off bark on branches and trunks, eat fruits and chew buds on trees and shrubs. They are pernicious and are at their worst where gardens border onto woodland. **What to do** Fit plastic tree-guards to newly planted trees to protect trunks; once completely girdled, a tree soon dies. Grow dwarf fruit trees in fruit cages formed of strong wire-netting.

Safety first with garden chemicals

Chemicals sprayed on plants in gardens are lethal to pests and therefore must be treated with respect.

- Carefully follow the manufacturer's instructions. Do not be tempted to use chemicals at higher than recommended concentrations as they will not be more effective, and may even damage plants.

- Do not spray near garden ponds, or where family rabbits and guinea pigs are kept and especially if in open runs and cages.

- Do not mix two different chemicals, unless recommended.

- Before using, check that the chemical will not damage specific plants.

- Keep all chemicals away from children and pets, and do not transfer chemicals into bottles that children might believe to be a refreshing drink.

- Do not use the same equipment for both weedkillers and insecticides.

- Thoroughly wash all spraying equipment after use, and store in a place not frequented by children or animals.

HOW TO AVOID GETTING PESTS AND DISEASES

Inspect new plants ~ see below right.

Inspect established plants regularly ~ for the presence of pests and diseases.

Regularly prune shrubs that require pruning ~ see pages 66–67. Shrubs that become congested, with masses of leaves and old stems, are particularly susceptible to pest and disease infestations.

Never leave rubbish lying about on the soil ~ remove prunings and dead flowers as soon as possible. They encourage the presence of pests.

Keep the soil free from weeds ~ they encourage the presence of pests.

Thoroughly prepare the soil ~ before planting a shrub or tree. Dig deeply and ensure good drainage, at the same time removing perennial weeds and exposing soil pests such as cockchafer grubs to birds.

CANKERS ON TREES

Canker is a general term for any kind of open wound on shrubs and trees, as well as other plants. Cankers usually appear as sunken, deformed areas on limbs and trunks and are caused by a number of different fungi. Examination indicates successive layers of dead tissue, with the tree making yearly attempts to grow over the originally damaged and infected area.

Bacterial canker is a serious disease of fruiting cherries, plums, peaches and Ornamental Cherries. Infection is likely to occur during autumn and winter, when spores enter wounds. Therefore, only prune these trees when their sap is rising. Paint wounds with a fungicidal tree paint.

Let the buyer beware!

When buying a shrub or tree, thoroughly check it to ensure it is free from pests and diseases. Look under leaves, as well as from above and especially around flowers and young shoots. Always buy plants from reputable sources.

Glossary

Arborescens Having a tree-like form.

Balled plants Mainly conifers or small evergreen shrubs with hessian tightly wrapped around the rootball. They are usually sold during late summer and early autumn, or in spring.

Bamboo Collective name for a wide range of plants in the grass family. They have stiff canes (some attractively coloured or shaped) and beautiful leaves (often brightly coloured).

Bare-rooted plants Deciduous shrubs or trees dug up from a nursery bed in winter, when they are bare of leaves.

Callus Tissue that forms over a wound, usually creating a raised surface.

Cambium Layer of growth and division that is just below the bark of shrubs and trees.

Clone A group of identical plants which have been raised vegetatively from a single, original parent.

Columnar Upright and narrow. Often used to describe some conifers.

Container gardening Growing plants – including shrubs and trees – in containers, perhaps on a patio or terrace.

Container-grown plants Plants growing in containers and ready for sale. They can be evergreen or deciduous shrubs and trees, for planting at any time of the year when the soil and weather are suitable.

Cultivar A variety raised in cultivation, rather than appearing naturally without any interference from man.

Deadheading The removal of faded flowerheads to prevent the formation of seeds and to encourage a plant to direct its energies into growth.

Deciduous Shrubs and trees (and some conifers) that shed their leaves in autumn and produce a fresh array in spring.

Dormant A resting period, normally in late autumn and winter, when a plant makes no noticeable growth.

Ericaceous Plants belonging to the Ericaceae family and including Heathers, Heaths, Ericas and Daboecias.

Evergreen Plants that appear to retain their leaves throughout the year and therefore are always green. However, they regularly lose leaves, while producing others.

Flower A specialized part of seed-bearing plants and concerned with reproduction.

Form A loose and non-botanical term referring to a variation within a particular species.

Fruit Botanically, a mature ovary bearing ripe seeds. Fruits can be soft and fleshy, or dry.

Glaucous Blue or grey-green and usually used to describe leaves and stems.

Hardy Able to survive winter outdoors in a temperate climate.

Heath Botanically, types of ericaceous plants, such as *Erica ciliaris* (Dorset Heath) and *Erica tetralix* (Cross-leaved Heath).

Heeling-in Covering the roots of bare-rooted trees while waiting to be planted.

H-stake A method of supporting standard trees, using two vertical stakes and one across the top, to which the trunk is secured.

Hybrid A plant resulting from a cross between two distinct varieties, species or genera.

Laciniata Fringed, and usually used to describe the edges and outlines of leaves or flowers.

Leader The main stem – or several – of trees and shrubs.

Mulching Covering the soil around trees and shrubs – and other plants – with well-decayed organic material such as garden compost and manure.

Oblique stake A method of supporting the trunk of a tree. A stake is inserted into the ground at a 45° angle, after a tree is planted.

Palmate Used to describe leaves that resemble the shape of a hand.

Petal Part of a flower and, botanically, a modified leaf, usually coloured. It creates a landing place for pollinating insects as well as attracting them through its colour and scent. When in bud, it acts as a protective layer for the flower's reproductive parts.

Pollard Cutting a tree hard back to near its trunk, usually because of the lack of surrounding space.

Pruning The controlled removal of stems and shoots to encourage a plant to form a better shape, develop fruits and flowers and, in a few instances, produce attractive stems.

Pyramidal Having the shape of a pyramid and often used to describe the shapes of trees and conifers.

Shrub A woody plant with several stems coming from ground level.

Specimen plant A plant that is grown on its own to create a special display or feature.

Standard A plant grown on a single stem, with a long, bare area between the ground and the lowest branches. Many fruit trees and roses – as well as ornamental trees – are grown as standards.

Stooling Cutting down woody stems to just above soil level to encourage the development of fresh shoots. A few shrubs and trees are regularly treated in this way, such as some Willows and Dogwoods.

Tree A woody-stemmed plant with a clear stem (trunk) between the roots and the lowest branches.

Tree-tie A method of securing a trunk to a support. Some are plastic; earlier, thick coir string was used. The tie must be adjustable to allow for expansion of the trunk.

Trunk The main stem of a tree.

Variegated Mainly applied to leaves and used to describe a state of having two or more colours.

Variety A naturally occurring variation with a plant.

Vertical stake A method of supporting a tree by inserting a stake vertically into the ground before it is planted. If inserted afterwards, the roots of the tree might be damaged.

Weeping Having a weeping nature and used to describe the outline of a tree or conifer. Some roses are grown as weeping standards, as well as ornamental trees.

Index

Acknowledgments

Photographs: AG&G Books (cover and pages 2, 3, 12, 69, 46TR, 47BR, 52, 54CL, 62BL, 63 and 64BR), Garden World Images (page 37TR), Peter McHoy (pages 18BL, 19TR, 22BC, 30BC, 31BL, 33TL, 37BC, 38, 39TC, 41C, 42, 43BC, 44 and 45TL), and David Squire (all pictures except those listed here).